# Counselling in general practice

Psychological and psychiatric disorders are the third most common diagnosis in consultations in primary care, following respiratory and cardiovascular disorders. Many general practitioners now employ counsellors to help them with the psychological and emotional problems of their patients. This book explores the counsellor's role in general practice and investigates the issues involved.

The contributors – GPs, counsellors and researchers – have wide experience of counsellor attachments and have been involved in developing and promoting GP counselling on a nation-wide scale. They discuss the extent of psychiatric and psychological disorders in primary care, and explain in detail what counselling is, and its ethics. They describe how to set up a counselling service in general practice and how to evaluate it, with examples of questionnaires. There are two detailed accounts of counselling attachments and a chapter on practical and training issues, which includes guidance on employing a counsellor and the issues to consider when setting up an attachment.

Intended as a guide for GPs, counsellors and practice nurses, and for Family Health Service Authority managers and planners, *Counselling in General Practice* will be of enormous help in enabling the primary care team to make the best use of its resources.

# Counselling in general practice

Edited by Roslyn Corney and
Rachel Jenkins

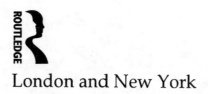

London and New York

MT

First published 1993
by Routledge
11 New Fetter Lane, London EC4P 4EE

Simultaneously published in the USA and Canada
by Routledge
29 West 35th Street, New York, NY 10001

Reprinted 1995

A Tavistock/Routledge publication

Typeset in Palatino by LaserScript Limited, Mitcham, Surrey
Printed and bound in Great Britain by
Biddles Ltd, Guildford and King's Lynn

*British Library Cataloguing in Publication Data*
A catalogue record for this book is available from the British Library.

*Library of Congress Cataloguing in Publication Data*
A catalogue record for this book is available from the Library of
Congress.

ISBN 0–415–05956–9

12/22/04

# Contents

# Tables

# Contributors

**Vivienne Ball** is primary care facilitator for Derbyshire FHSA and a practising counsellor in general practice. She has worked in primary care for eight years initially as a health visitor and then as a counsellor. She is Chair of the Counselling in General Practice Sub-group of the BAC and Chair of the National Working Party for the Development of Guidelines for Counselling in General Practice.

**Roslyn Corney** is a senior lecturer at the Institute of Psychiatry and in the Centre for Health Service Studies at the University of Kent at Canterbury. A psychologist by training, she has conducted a number of clinical trials of counselling. Her research interests include the evaluation of attachments of social workers and counsellors to general practice, investigating help seeking and illness behaviour, and developing the skills of primary care practitioners in the identification and management of psychological and emotional problems. She has recently edited a book published by Routledge called *Developing Communication and Counselling Skills in Medicine* aimed at developing the skills of all clinicians involved in medical care.

**Annalee Curran** works as a counsellor in an inner London general practice. She is also a trainer and supervisor in Cognitive Analytic Therapy (CAT) and is involved in a number of community counselling projects. She has run groups for counsellors and GPs for the Department of General Practice and Primary Care at King's College Hospital and is currently part of a project team in that department working with the Open University to devise a course on Mental Health.

**Raanan Gillon** is Director of the Imperial College Health Service, Visiting Professor of Medical Ethics at St Mary's Hospital Medical School and Editor of the *Journal of Medical Ethics.*

**Roger Higgs** is a general practitioner in south London and Professor in the Department of General Practice and Primary Care at King's College Hospital. He started as a single-handed GP, and has been involved with a number of new projects, including the creation of a new type of GP hospital (the Lambeth Community Care Centre) and the development of local services, including counselling. His academic interests include medical ethics, shared medical care and psychosocial issues in practice, and he has written *In That Case – Medical Ethics in Everyday Practice* with Alastair Campbell.

**Jill Irving** began counselling in 1968 and went on to train and supervise counsellors for the National Marriage Guidance Council. After studying psychology at Brunel University and spending some time in research she resumed counselling and worked in a general practice for several years. Through the British Association for Counselling she has helped with the production of guidelines and information on the employment of counsellors in general practice and has published articles on counselling in general practice in both the counselling and medical press. At present she is working as a counsellor in the NHS and at a private clinic in Berkshire.

**Rachel Jenkins** is Honorary Senior Lecturer at the Institute of Psychiatry and Principal Medical Officer at the Mental Health, Elderly and Disability Unit, Department of Health, London.

**Anthony Mann** is the Professor of Epidemiological Psychiatry, Institute of Psychiatry and Royal Free Hospital School of Medicine. He was formerly a senior lecturer at the Royal Free Hospital School of Medicine. His main interests have been the epidemiological study of mental disorders of old age, of psychiatric aspects of cardiovascular disease and in psychiatry in primary care settings.

**Geoffrey N. Marsh** has worked in a primary health care team at Norton Medical Centre, Stockton on Tees, for 30 years. For at least 20 of those he has had a counsellor working as one of the team members. Dr Marsh has been a visiting professor at the University of Iowa, USA, and also Wolfson travelling professor in Canada for the Royal College of General Practitioners.

epidemiological study of mental disorders of old age, of psychiatric aspects of cardiovascular disease and in psychiatry in primary care settings.

**Geoffrey N. Marsh** has worked in a primary health care team at Norton Medical Centre, Stockton on Tees, for 30 years. For at least 20 of those he has had a counsellor working as one of the team members. Dr Marsh has been a visiting professor at the University of Iowa, USA, and also Wolfson travelling professor in Canada for the Royal College of General Practitioners.

**Nancy Rowland** is a counsellor and researcher. She is currently evaluating the cost-effectiveness of counselling at the Centre for Health Economics at the University of York. Her special interest is in counselling in clinical settings and she chairs the Counselling in Medical Settings Division of the British Association for Counselling.

# Preface

Psychological and psychiatric disorders are the third most common diagnosis in consultations in primary care, closely following respiratory disorders (15 per cent) and cardiovascular disorders (11 per cent). As long ago as 1966, Shepherd and colleagues demonstrated that 14 per cent of consultations in general practice have an identified psychological component, and that most of this morbidity is depression and anxiety.

A simple look at the logistics of general practice makes it clear that the general practitioner cannot handle this alone. The challenge, therefore, is to see how best the primary care team can be deployed to meet this huge task and what resources can be used to supplement and support the team.

Recently, the most frequent resource used by GPs to tackle non-psychotic psychiatric morbidity is the use of counsellors, who are often employed directly by the GP to take referrals within the practice. This development has grown remarkably rapidly over the last few years, and the time is ripe to examine closely the role of counsellors in general practice. This book has been conceived and written in an attempt to provide a detailed account of the issues surrounding counselling in general practice today, and arose from a National Conference on Counselling in General Practice held in May 1989. It is a guide for general practitioners, counsellors and other members of the primary care team.

The book includes chapters on the research showing the extent of psychiatric and psychological disorders in primary care, a more detailed description of what counselling is, the ethics of counselling, details of whether counselling has been shown to bring about client improvement and how to evaluate a counselling attachment. The book also includes two accounts of counselling attachments and a chapter on practical and training issues, which also includes practical guidance on employing a counsellor and the issues that need to be considered when setting up an attachment.

# Acknowledgements

The idea of a book arose from a conference in May 1989 organised by the Institute of Psychiatry on Counselling in Primary Care. The conference, sponsored by the Department of Health, was chaired by Dr John Horder and Professor Roger Higgs. We would also like to thank Julie Smith for her conscientious typing of the manuscripts.

# Chapter 1

# Counselling in general practice today

*Roslyn Corney and Rachel Jenkins*

Approximately one-third of all patients who consult their GP are likely to be seeking help for the emotional distress associated with a physical illness, or for what can be termed a 'life problem'. Patients with emotional problems have been shown to attend their GP more frequently and show an increased demand for other medical services. In addition, studies have shown that patients with psychosocial problems are more likely to turn to a GP rather than the psychiatric or social services. In consequence, the majority of emotional problems experienced by patients are treated by GPs or by another member of the primary care team without referral to the mental health services. These details are documented in greater detail in Chapter 2.

A range of other professionals support and help GPs with these patients. These include other members of the primary care team, health visitors, district nurses and practice nurses as well as attachments of other professionals in the mental health field, such as psychologists, community psychiatric nurses and psychiatrists. More recently, counsellor attachments have also been set up specifically for this purpose.

## THE DEVELOPMENT OF THE PRIMARY HEALTH CARE TEAM

Following the Family Doctor Charter of 1966, GPs were encouraged to form group practices and the number of single-handed doctors began to fall. This has proceeded steadily until the present day when most young doctors entering general practice join a group practice. The Department of Health has also encouraged the building of group practice centres by offering favourable loans and rent schemes and by the provision of local authority-owned health centres. Approximately 25 per cent of general practitioners now work in such health centres.

In parallel with the development of premises came the attachment of District Health Authority nursing staff, to group practices and health centres in the 1960s (health visitors, district nurses and midwives). Ancillary staff, including receptionists, secretaries and administrators, had 70 per cent of their salaries paid by the local Family Practitioner Committee (FPC), and each doctor was able to have one or two staff members funded in this way.

In 1975, Marsh first reported on the work of a counsellor in general practice and, since then, a number of attachments have been described in the literature. However, the funding of these attachments has always been a problem. Originally many counsellors gave their services free or charged the client directly (usually on a scale according to the client's financial circumstances). In a few instances, the GPs paid the counsellors while other counsellors claimed their fees from the patient's private health insurance (if referred via a psychiatrist). More recently, however, some FPCs have been willing to fund counsellor attachments using the ancillary staff scheme described above. In July 1989, the British Association for Counselling asked all 94 FPCs if they were employing counsellors in general practice. Of the 52 who responded, 52 per cent were currently using counsellors and 42 per cent had agreed to reimburse GPs from the ancillary staff scheme.

A new contract for GPs came into operation in April 1990 and brought about a number of changes, some of which have made it easier for GPs to fund counsellors in general practice. Since the new GP contract, the range of staff eligible for reimbursement has been extended so that staff (including counsellors) who have a wider range of skills and training also qualify. However, the new contract does not guarantee that practices will continue to receive 70 per cent reimbursement of staff salaries through the ancillary scheme (except those staff in post prior to April 1990). Other GPs, however, have been using the money received through their health promotion clinics to pay counsellors. In this event, the counsellors have organised their counselling sessions as health promotion clinics – promoting mental health and preventing mental illness/breakdown – and are therefore eligible to claim money specifically set aside for this purpose.

The FPCs have been taken over by the Family Health Service Authorities (FHSAs). These FHSAs have new powers and are entitled to vet any counsellors employed by GPs to ensure that they are suitably trained and experienced.

## THE ROLE OF THE GP AS COUNSELLOR

McLeod (1992) stated that the 'work of the GPs has always included counselling whether this is seen as the application of counselling skills in the consultation or the informed use of the counselling process with selected patients'; but the majority of doctors enter general practice with little training in counselling. This lack of preparation for counselling 'together with the very real constraints of time, has limited the capacity of many GPs to adequately recognise patients' needs and to respond effectively to these needs' (McLeod,1992).

The potential of the consultation in general practice was explored by Michael Balint and his followers. Balint groups have been established where small groups of doctors develop effective ways of using short consultations. The skills and techniques of counselling are an important and necessary part of the work of all GPs, as they are constantly involved in their patients' grief after a bereavement, their relationship difficulties, children's problems after a marital breakup, or those learning to cope with a chronic or serious illness. 'Listening sensitively to the patient and helping to make sense of his distress, the use of explanation, guidance and informed reassurance are all "tools of the trade"' (McLeod, 1992).

Counsellors and others argue that although counselling skills help the GPs in their consultations, the focus of the doctor's work is different from that of the counsellor (Rowland et al., 1989). In general, the aim and function of a counsellor is to help the clients to help themselves, to clarify difficulties and attempt to resolve them. Rather than giving advice, reassurance or medication, the counsellor systematically attempts to avoid long-term dependency. The GP's role is sometimes different; the GP can be viewed as the expert, whose job is to listen to the patient, attempt to diagnose any disorder and prescribe treatment to ease or to cure. Even those GPs who have trained as counsellors do not always find it easy to enter into this sort of counselling relationship or to have the time or emotional resources to do so. There may also be problems for which they have to revert to a 'doctoring' role at a later stage (Rowland *et al.*, 1989).

## SHOULD COUNSELLING BE OFFERED IN PRIMARY CARE?

### Advantages

A number of favourable accounts of counselling attachments that have been published in the general practice and counselling literature are reviewed in Chapter 4. The lack of unfavourable accounts (published or unpublished) may indicate that they are rare occurrences or that they have not been documented formally (or a combination of the two).

Reports of successful attachment and employment schemes of other professionals (Clare and Corney, 1982; Strathdee, 1988) have shown that these schemes generally facilitate better collaboration and communication and the development of trust between different professionals. Doctors feel happier at referring distressed patients to someone whom they know and trust. The doctor might also receive direct feedback from referred patients.

Counsellor attachments may also benefit the counsellor who might gain satisfaction from being part of a team rather than working in isolation in addition to the medical support and back-up provided (Corney, 1987).

As shall be discussed in Chapter 3, a counsellor in the practice may also offer support to other members of the team. This may enable team members to undertake some of the counselling work. Sharing the care of patients with long-term intractable problems may help reduce the stress imposed by these patients.

Many GPs consider that one advantage of employing counsellors is that clients can see a counsellor in a familiar environment. The fact that the doctor has suggested counselling may overcome the client's initial scepticism of the value of counselling. Being referred to an 'in-house counsellor' might not attract the same stigma as a psychiatric referral. In addition, one of the problems of referring patients to psychiatrists is that many patients fail to turn up for the first appointment (Illman, 1983).

**Disadvantages**

One of the main disadvantages is that of cost. The costs of employing a qualified counsellor are not inconsiderable and we have little evidence (as yet) to indicate whether clients benefit greatly from professional counselling in comparison to other forms of 'talking' help. Would a harassed and depressed young mother receive as much benefit from talking to a health visitor (with limited counselling training) as talking to a counsellor? Would the support and befriending from another young mother with slightly older children be as helpful?

Counsellors are limited in the number of clients that can be seen each week and it is important that each referral is considered carefully. Other options such as group counselling or making more use of the counsellor's role in supporting and advising other members of the primary care team should also be considered to limit excessive costs.

The question of client choice has also to be considered. Attaching counsellors to primary care may limit client choice. Some clients may regard that being referred to a counsellor in a general practice 'may not provide sufficient anonymity and privacy' (McLeod, 1988). It is important that other options are available for clients who wish to seek alternative help that is not linked to medical care. Many doctors would argue that employing counsellors has far-reaching consequences as it legitimises general practice as the place to go with social and emotional problems. Will the widespread adoption of counsellors employed in general practice increase the medicalisation of these social and emotional problems? Or will patients feel that they do not have to adopt a sick role (and accompanying illness behaviours) to visit their GP with these problems before being referred to more appropriate help?

## CONCLUSION

A number of questions will be raised in the following chapters. However, it is vital that future counselling placements are properly and systematically evaluated so that firmer evidence is obtained on the benefits and costs of providing counsellors in this setting.

## REFERENCES

Clare, A. W. and Corney, R. H. (1982) *Social Work and Primary Health Care*, London: Academic Press.

Corney, R. (1987) 'Marriage guidance counselling in general practice in London', *British Journal of Guidance and Counselling* 15: 50–8.

Illman, J. (1983) 'Is psychiatric referral good value for money?', *BMA New Review* 9: 41–2.

McLeod, J (1988) *The Work of Counsellors in General Practice*, Occasional Paper 37, London: Royal College of General Practitioners.

McLeod, J. (1992) 'Counselling in primary health care, the GP's perspective', in M. Sheldon (ed.), *Royal College of General Practitioners Clinical Series on Counselling in General Practice*, London: RCGP Enterprises.

Marsh, G.N. and Barr, J. (1975) 'Marriage guidance counselling in a group practice', *Journal of the Royal College of General Practitioners* 25: 73–5.

Rowland, N., Irving, J. and Maynard, A. K.(1989) 'Can GPs counsel?', *Journal of the Royal College of General Practitioners* 39: 118–20.

Strathdee, G. (1988) 'Psychiatrists in primary care: the general practitioner viewpoint', *Family Practice* 5: 111–15.

# Chapter 2

# The need for counselling

## The extent of psychiatric and psychosocial disorders in primary care – a review of the epidemiological research findings

*Anthony Mann*

Psychiatric and psychosocial disorders seen and managed within primary care settings can easily be belittled; the critics adopting several arguments, including:

> Compared to many common physical diseases, psychiatric disorders and psychosocial problems seen in primary care do not constitute a major health issue.
> They are not 'real' mental illnesses.
> Nothing much is known and anyway most of these disorders recover spontaneously.

The purpose of this chapter is to respond to such observations. The evidence quoted is largely drawn from work carried out over the last two decades within the former General Practice Research Unit, under the direction of Professor Michael Shepherd, at the Institute of Psychiatry.

### ARE THEY A PUBLIC HEALTH ISSUE?

Epidemiological studies, both here and in the United States, suggest that the rate of mental illness in the population is in the range 10–15 per cent at any point in time. These figures can be enlarged or reduced, depending on the extent and duration of symptoms counted and whether those disorders associated with physical illnesses are included. All such community surveys show that the non-psychotic disorders – anxiety and depression – are the most prevalent. The important and relevant item is that the primary care service in the United Kingdom is the main point of contact for people with psychiatric disorders.

Over double the number of contacts occur for psychiatric

*Table 2.1* Comparative rates of attendance for different levels of psychiatric care (rates per 100,000 general population, all ages and sexes combined in 1981)

|  | General practitioner consultations * | Outpatients attendances ‡ | Day hospital attendances ‡ | Psychiatric admissions ‡ |
|---|---|---|---|---|
| ICD–9 290–315 Mental disorders | 22,980 | 3,532 | 4,943 | 397 |

\* Obtained from: *Morbidity Statistics from General Practice 1981–1982*
‡ Obtained from: *Mental Health Inquiry for England*, 1981
*Source*: Sharp and Morrell (1988)

disorder in primary care compared to other forms of psychiatric contact. *National Morbidity Statistics* show that, at 9 per cent, psychiatric disorders rank as the third most common cause of consultation in primary care following those to do with the respiratory system at 15 per cent and those to do with the cardiovascular system at 11 per cent. Tables 2.2 and 2.3 show that it is the non-psychotic psychiatric disorders that produce the work for general practitioners. These data are drawn from Shepherd's study (Shepherd et al., 1966) and from a paper published by the Royal College of General Practitioners (RCGP, 1973).

In answer then to the first critical comment, these figures – which are available to anyone – demonstrate the scale of the public health problem posed by the non-psychotic psychiatric disorders.

*Table 2.2* Psychiatric disorder in an average general practice population of 2,500

| Acute major disorders | Cases per annum |
|---|---|
| Severe depression | 12 |
| Suicide attempts | 3 |
| Completed suicide | One every 3 years |
| Chronic mental illness | 55 |
| Severe mental handicap | 10 |
| Neurotic disorders | 300 |

*Source*: RCGP (1973)

Table 2.3 Patients' consulting rates per 1,000 at risk for psychiatric morbidity, by sex and diagnostic group

| Diagnostic group | Male | Female | Both sexes |
|---|---|---|---|
| Psychoses | 2.7 | 8.6 | 5.9 |
| Mental subnormality | 1.6 | 2.9 | 2.3 |
| Dementia | 1.2 | 1.6 | 1.4 |
| Neuroses | 55.7 | 116.6 | 88.5 |
| Personality disorder | 7.2 | 4.0 | 5.5 |
| Formal psychiatric illness* | 67.2 | 131.9 | 102.1 |
| Psychosomatic conditions | 24.5 | 34.5 | 29.9 |
| Organic illness with psychiatric overlay | 13.1 | 16.6 | 15.0 |
| Psychosocial problems | 4.6 | 10.0 | 7.5 |
| Psychiatric-associated conditions* | 38.6 | 57.2 | 48.6 |
| Total psychiatric morbidity* | 97.9 | 175.0 | 139.4 |
| Number of patients at risk | 6,783 | 7,914 | 14,697 |

* These totals cannot be obtained by adding the rates for the relevant diagnostic groups because while a patient may be included in more than one diagnostic group, he or she will be included only once in the total.
Source: Shepherd et al. (1966)

## ARE SUFFERERS REALLY ILL?

A statement that these disorders are 'not really mental illness' would imply that they do not warrant attention by a health care professional nor warrant Department of Health resources. They can be labelled as the 'minor' psychiatric syndromes, or sufferers may be called the 'walking worried'. Such judgements can be countered by three different types of evidence which indicate that these disorders can be severe, both for the provision of health care and for the patients.

The first evidence is clinical. Studies have taken place that have compared the symptomatology of depression and anxiety (the most common diagnoses) in different settings to contradict the critic who says that the consulters in general practice are just discontented, distressed or not coping with life, and do not match clinical depression as seen in hospital populations. Both Brown and colleagues (1985) and Blacker and Clare (1987) have demonstrated an overlap in symptomatology and severity. Many very severe depressions are referred to hospital settings, to concentrate in front of the psychiatrist. This gives the hospital psychiatrist the impression that the depressive condition he or she is seeing is somehow different from those in general practice. However, such severe depressions are to be found among general practice attenders – 5 per cent of consultations for depression – albeit diluted by milder states of anxiety and depression.

The association between successful suicide and a recent consultation with a medical doctor also suggests that among these consulters are some very severely depressed people. Of course, in the end what is called severe and therefore true mental illness stems from a personal or professional group judgement. It is quite possible to set criteria, so that only patients with the most obviously depressive mental state are called ill, and those that are otherwise complaining are called miserable. However, criteria should in the end take into account the impact of these states on patients' lives.

There are two other forms of evidence that warrant scrutiny. First, what actions have the general practitioners taken to try to treat these disorders? The general practitioners have regarded that some form of medication is necessary. It is clear from the figures of prescriptions dispensed at retail pharmacies in England that massive prescribing activity in terms of tranquillisers and antidepressants have occurred following the arrival and the marketing of psychotropic drugs.

Table 2.4 shows the economic effect of these disorders – increasingly used as an indicator of severity. This table shows the economic costs of the non-psychotic disorders as seen in general practice, costing the actual expense of the time and treatment involved, and then the impact of these disorders upon the patients' economic functioning. The total sum is vast.

*Table 2.4*  Costs of neurotic disorder in general practice

| | | |
|---|---|---|
| Consultations and drug costs | £119.5 | million |
| Costs of sickness absence | £253 | million |
| *Total* (minimal estimate) | £373 | million |
| plus:    Cost of early retirement | £2,700 | million |
| Uncertificated sickness absence | £2,900 | million |
| **Total cost of neurosis in general practice**    = | £6,000,000,000 | |

*Source*:    Croft-Jeffreys and Wilkinson, 1989

## WHAT IS KNOWN ABOUT THESE DISORDERS?

The first fact is that all published statistics concern only those people recognised by the general practitioner, at consultation, as suffering from psychiatric disorders. Goldberg and Huxley (1980) initiated the concepts of *conspicuous morbidity* (those sufferers known to practitioners), and *hidden morbidity* (those not known), the proportion being approximately one to one.

The problem for primary care personnel is probably even larger than Tables 2.1–2.4 suggest; there being another group of patients passing through the practice suffering from these syndromes, but not being so recorded. A second fact is the effect of age and sex distribution of consulters.

Table 2.5 shows, by age and sex, a typical set of 100 people consulting general practitioners, with the general practitioner's diagnosis drawn from the *National Morbidity Statistics*. This typical cohort shows that the commonest diagnoses among its members are anxiety and depression and the commonest age group is between 25 and 55. There is a sex bias among consulters to primary care: 2.5 women to 1 male. This may be an underestimation of the consulters in the older age band as these figures are based upon conspicuous morbidity – a syndrome that may be under-recognised in older people. For instance, in a recent survey of elderly residents in the community in north London, 17 per cent of the pensioners were classed as clinically depressed, 27 per cent with significant depressive symptoms (Livingston *et al.*, 1990). Over half of these had consulted their general practitioner in the preceding month, yet only one in eight of the depressed were receiving antidepressant medication.

Table 2.6 is drawn from a research study in which general practitioners' assessments of the psychiatric disorders in primary care were compared with those of a psychiatrist who had interviewed the same patients and it shows the comparison of general practitioners' and psychiatrist's diagnoses. The study found that general practitioners are diagnosing real psychiatric illnesses and that they did not diagnose psychiatric illness where the psychiatrist finds none. Although the psychiatrists tend to diagnose more depression in preference to anxiety, there was a considerable degree of agreement between them.

Psychiatric disorders in primary care settings are associated, both at time of presentation and in the lifetime of an individual,

Table 2.5 Outcome of neurotic illness in general practice*

| | (a) General practitioner's diagnosis | | | | | | | | | (b) |
| | Women (N = 72) | | | | Men (N = 28) | | | | Total | Psychiatrist's diagnosis |
| | 15–24 | 25–44 | 45–64 | 65+ | 15–24 | 25–44 | 45–64 | 65+ | | |
|---|---|---|---|---|---|---|---|---|---|---|
| Anxiety neurosis/ phobic neurosis | 3 | 9 | 8 | 3 | 1 | 4 | 4 | 1 | 33 | 33 |
| Depressive neurosis | 3 | 11 | 10 | 5 | 1 | 3 | 4 | 1 | 38 | 56 |
| Physical disorders of psychogenic origin/tension headache | 2 | 5 | 4 | 1 | 1 | 2 | 2 | 0 | 17 | 3 |
| Insomnia | 0 | 1 | 1 | 1 | 0 | 0 | 1 | 1 | 5 | 2 |
| Other conditions | 1 | 2 | 1 | 1 | 0 | 1 | 1 | 0 | 7 | 6 |
| Total | 9 | 28 | 24 | 11 | 3 | 10 | 12 | 3 | 100 | 100 |

* The composition of a cohort calculated to be representative of patients attending general practitioners with non-psychotic psychiatric disorders from the *National Morbidity Statistics* (HMSO), 1974.

with the concurrent presence of physical illness. Clusterings of illnesses of both types, psychiatric and physical, tend to occur in the same individuals. Eastwood and Trevelyan (1972) showed this was a significant association, which has been confirmed in other forms in subsequent cross-section and longitudinal studies. There are several implications of this research finding. Here is a common cause for missed psychiatric disorder in primary care, because the coexisting physical disease dominates the diagnosis. Secondly, the management of the psychiatric state must take physical status into account. Thirdly, there may be implications for the understanding of the genesis of these disorders. Are changes in body function and mental function linked in the same way?

Other work has shown the relationship to social stresses. Cooper and Sylph (1973) showed that the patients attending primary care with neurotic disorders had much more evidence of social adversity, such as limited and difficult relationships, and less satisfaction with their occupation and other practical aspects of life. These ideas have been further developed by Brown and Harris (1978), who have taken such associations and developed a model for depression in the community in which knowledge of personal vulnerability and adverse events can provide an explanation for who gets depressed. Henderson (1981) has taken further the concept of social network and its impairment. With standard assessment, Henderson first showed that the neurotic patient had fewer contacts and therefore a poorer network than the non-neurotic, but later research eventually determined that it wasn't the actual extent of the network that mattered, but perceived quality. Those with neurotic disorders perceived a much poorer quality of support around them than those without.

## DO THESE PATIENTS RECOVER ANYWAY?

Relatively little research has been carried out on the natural history of these disorders in primary care. First, few are referred: 5 per cent. For the remainder, the general clinical impression has been that many clear up, but that some significant proportion may become protracted illnesses. Mann *et al.* (1981) conducted a follow-up study in two general practices in the Midlands of 100 patients selected by the general practitioner as suffering from non-psychotic illness who, by dint of their age, sex and diagnosis were representative of those consulting general practitioners in the country (see Table 2.6). This typical cohort was assessed in detail, their general practice contact over the following year was monitored and a reassessment took place one year later. The two assessments by the psychiatrist consisted not only of their psychiatric symptoms, but also of their perceived stresses and support in the social environment and of their personality, as reported at an interview by an informant.

At one year, 52 per cent of the cohort of 100 patients had recovered. Analysis of the initial assessment indicated that factors found to be important were the initial severity of symptoms, perceived poor quality of social life, perceived poor quality of marriage and being prescribed a psychotropic drug. Thus, patients with initially high clinical scores, on psychotropic drugs, with poor marriages and poor quality social lives were more likely to be still depressed at one year.

It can be seen from Table 2.6 that only a quarter showed a rapid recovery in the early months of the follow-up year and didn't relapse (group (a)); about a half had an intermittent course (group (b)), and a quarter had a chronic course with apparently regular consultations throughout the year (group (c)). Factors at outset, that were associated with membership of these groups, were sought. The first analysis compared the best outcome, group (a), with membership of groups (b) and (c) using a discriminant

*Table 2.6*  Neurotic illness in general practice: outcome at one year

| *Course* | (a) | 24 per cent rapid recovery |
|---|---|---|
| | (b) | 52 per cent remittent |
| | (c) | 24 per cent chronic course |

(a) vs (b) and (c)
Predicted by:  Perceived good quality social life I and II
                      Perceived good quality family support I
                      Not receiving psychotropic medication

(c) vs (a) and (b)
Predicted by:  Receiving psychotropic drugs
                      Significant physical illness
                      More severe symptom state

*Source* :  Mann *et al.* (1981)

function analysis. The earlier recoverers were characterised by: perception of good quality of social life at years one and two, perceived good quality of family support at outset and not receiving psychotropic medication. A second analysis compared membership of group (c) with the other two groups, (a) and (b). Receiving a psychotropic drug, presence of significant physical illness and a more severe symptom state at onset characterised this group.

This study shows that, even in the setting of a research study in a prosperous area of the country, a quarter of people consulting with conspicuous morbidity have a chronic course with perpetual complaint, regular consultation and poor outcome one year later and a further half seem to have a remitting course. Receipt of medication was not associated with a rapid recovery. This chronic subgroup has also been recognised in the United States (Regier *et al.*, 1985). They make up a persistent, constant load for the general practitioner in time spent in consultation and, it would seem, receive much medication. Yet if this study is to be believed, one can see that perception of good qualities of support, both in marriage, in family and in the social network, are the factors that are associated with rapid recovery. Thus a case can be made for interventions, other than medical, to help people improve their social supports.

## CONCLUSION

The non-psychotic disorders of primary care are a major public health problem because of their clinical severity and their high economic cost. Research has begun to unravel some of the factors which precipitate and maintain these illnesses. Despite much pharmacological activity, they still contribute to the chronic ill health of the population. Development of interventions that foster social adjustment and improved coping mechanisms would seem an important way forward.

## REFERENCES

Blacker, C. V. R. and Clare, A. W. (1987) 'Depressive disorder in primary care', *British Journal of Psychiatry* 150: 3–51.

Brown, G. W. and Harris, T. (1978) *Social Origins of Depression: a Study of Psychiatric Disorder in Women*, London: Tavistock.

Brown, G. W., Craig, T. K. J. and Harris, T.O. (1985) 'Depression: disease or distress? Some epidemiological considerations', *British Journal of Psychiatry* 147: 612–22.

Cooper, B. and Sylph, J. (1973) 'Life events and the onset of neurotic illness: an investigation in general practice', *Psychological Medicine* 3: 421–35.

Croft-Jeffreys, C. and Wilkinson G. (1989) 'Estimated costs of neurotic disorder in UK general practice 1985', *Psychological Medicine* 19: 549–58.

Eastwood, M. R. and Trevelyan, M. H. (1972) 'Relationship between physical and psychiatric disorder', *Psychological Medicine* 2: 363–2.

Goldberg, D. P. and Huxley, P. (1980) *Mental Illness in the Community: the Pathway to Psychiatric Care,* London: Tavistock.

Henderson, S. (1981) 'Social relationships, adversity and neurosis: an analysis of prospective observations', *British Journal of Psychiatry* 138: 391–8.

Livingston, G., Hawkins, A., Graham, N., Blizard, R. and Mann, A. H. (1990) 'The Gospel Oak Study: prevalence rates of dementia, depression and activity limitation among elderly residents in inner London', *Psychological Medicine* 20: 13–146.

Mann, A., Jenkins, R. and Belsey, E. (1981) 'The outcome of neurotic illness in general practice', *Psychological Medicine* 11: 535–50.

Regier, D. A., Burke, J. D., Manderscheid, R. W. and Burns, B. J. (1985) 'The chronically mentally ill in primary care', *Psychological Medicine* 15: 265–73.

RCGP (1973) Present status and future needs of general practice, *Journal of the Royal College of General Practitioners,* Reports on general practice No.16.

Sharp, D. and Morrell, D. (1988) 'The psychiatry of general practice', in P. Williams *et al.* (eds), *The Scope of Epidemiological Psychiatry,* London: Routledge, pp. 404–19.

Shepherd, M., Cooper, B., Brown, A. C. and Kalton, G. W. (1966) *Psychiatric Illness in General Practice,* London: Oxford University Press.

Williams, P. and Clare, A. (1986) 'Psychiatry in general practice', in P. Hill, R. Murray and A. Thorley (eds), *Essentials of Postgraduate Psychiatry,* London: Grune and Stratton, pp. 597–622 (2nd edn).

# Chapter 3

# What is counselling?

*Nancy Rowland*

One of the most interesting articles on counselling written over the past couple of years is called 'Let's do away with counselling' by Harris (1987). In it he argues that counselling has replaced benzodiazepines as the major panacea for all ills, that it is difficult to understand what counsellors have to offer apart from 'time, sympathy and a willingness to help' and that these qualities appear to be more important in the counselling relationship than the theory or method of counselling. With no common understanding of what counselling means, there is no way in which its value can be assessed. 'We smile at old quack remedies which claimed to cure baldness, kidney stones, stammering, poor appetite, the ague, female complaints and dropsy, but the analogy is pretty close.' Harris thus concludes that 'we can . . . do very well without counselling'.

While there isn't much hope for the baby in Harris's bath water, the points he raises are valid. Time is often a scarce resource and counsellors working a 50-minute session have more time to offer than the busy GP who can give an average six minutes or arrange an extended consultation. But what makes the extra time counsellors offer valuable? As Harris points out, sympathy can be inhibiting or destructive and a willingness to help is not always associated with an ability to do so. Is counselling any different from tea and sympathy and a shoulder to cry on? What is counselling? Does it work? Who does it work best for? What is the difference between what a counsellor does in the therapeutic hour and what a GP does in the clinical consultation? The first part of this chapter aims to define counselling and to examine its constituent parts: the theory that underpins it;

the counsellor who practises it and the stages that structure the counselling process. The difference between counselling and counselling skills is stressed. The second part of the chapter examines the role of the counsellor in general practice, the types of clients counsellors see and the sort of work they do.

## WHAT IS COUNSELLING?

As Lindsay Knight (1986) points out, counselling has become a catch-word, used and misused in all walks of life. It has become a grand way of describing the giving of advice, so the woman who sells make-up is a beauty counsellor, the person who advises on matching curtains and wallpaper is called a colour counsellor. On a professional level, and without necessarily undergoing any training in counselling, some doctors claim to 'do all the counselling' in their practice, and surgery conversations in which the doctor 'counsels' the patient have an impressive sound to them which 'having a chat about it' lacks (Harris, 1987).

The misconceptions about counselling arise on two counts: (1) the dictionary defines counselling as synonymous with giving advice, whereas much of the counselling practised in Britain today is non-directive (in which the giving of advice is specifically barred); (2) there is a lack of understanding of the difference between counselling and the use of counselling skills. The difference between counselling and counselling skills is discussed in some detail below, but to start it's worth reiterating some of the things that counselling is not. So, it is not giving advice or information, persuasion or discipline. According to the British Association for Counselling (BAC, 1992),

> Counselling is the skilled and principled use of relationships to develop self knowledge, emotional acceptance and growth, and personal resources. The overall aim is to live more fully and satisfyingly. Counselling may be concerned with addressing and resolving specific problems, making decisions, coping with crisis, working through feelings or inner conflict or improving relationships with others. The counsellor's role is to facilitate the client's work in ways that respect the client's values, personal resources and capacity for self determination.

## TALKING CURES IN MEDICINE

At least four different therapeutic approaches are used in psychological medicine, each based on firm theoretical frameworks. These are psychoanalysis, psychotherapy, behavioural counselling and non-directive counselling (Williams, 1983). We are back once more at what counselling is not. Counselling is not psychoanalysis, which involves a practitioner trained in analytic theory using specific techniques such as free association, interpretation and transference. Psychoanalysis is intensive treatment lasting several years; it is rarely available on the NHS and usually costs a lot of money.

Psychotherapy also focuses on the transferential relationships between patient and therapist, although it uses a variety of other methods which distinguish it from psychoanalysis. The differences between psychotherapy and counselling are usually of orientation and degree rather than being fundamental to the two activities. In counselling there is less emphasis on, though not necessarily less awareness of, the transference between counsellor and client. Counselling tends to be shorter term and problem-centred, focusing on current personal difficulties and life problems, rather than analysis of the deep-seated personal problems dealt with in psychotherapy. While there is a great deal of overlap, it might be argued that the short-term, problem-centred counselling is better suited to general practice settings than psychotherapy. Williams (1983) puts it succinctly: 'Psychotherapy presumes treatment; there is a therapist and a patient, therefore there must be something to treat, for instance, a personality problem which requires change. Counselling on the other hand implies there is no treatment, although there is a problem.'

As its name suggests, behaviour therapy deals with the behaviour of the patient, such as smoking, drinking, phobia and so on. The techniques used are active and directive, and patients participate in a series of interventions aimed at modifying the maladaptive behaviour. By contrast, probably the most widely practised counselling model is non-directive counselling. Non-directive counsellors are trained not to advise clients but to help them make decisions for themselves. The counsellor respects the client as an equal and assumes that the client can, with help, resolve his or her difficulties. The counsellor aims to listen to and question the client to gain an understanding of how the client sees things, in the process enabling the client to clarify thoughts and feelings, generating a better understanding of his or her situation and with a fresh perspective, find a fresh approach to the problem.

## THEORIES OF COUNSELLING

Though non-directive counselling is perhaps the most widely practised model in Britain, many other theoretical models of counselling exist (Herink, in 1980, listed over 250) and the range and diversity of approach and the claims made about their effectiveness can be confusing for those seeking counselling, those seeking to employ a counsellor, or those seeking counselling training (Sutton, 1987). While it is beyond the scope of this chapter to evaluate the efficacy of different models, it is useful to note that, in practice, the variety of counselling models can be grouped into two different schools: directive and non-directive counselling. Active or directive counsellors tend to interpret, instruct and direct their clients, and reflective or non-directive counsellors tend to elicit and reflect, guide and support their clients (Irving and Heath, 1989).

To be effective, counsellors need a sound understanding of counselling theory capable of providing reliable guidelines for thinking and planning about counselling in general or for the moment-to-moment decisions of professional practice (Combs, 1989). Such theory embodies knowledge about the techniques of counselling, the function of the therapeutic alliance between counsellor and client and an appreciation of the relevance of the counsellor's attitudes and values in the counselling process, as well as an understanding of human development, and knowledge about society. Munro *et al.* (1983) recommend that those who undertake counselling should commit themselves to learning as much as possible about the factors involved in the process; subjective personal knowledge, and objective knowledge in the form of useful principles. Counselling theory and counsellor skills are fundamental to the counselling process.

## STAGES OF COUNSELLING

Egan's widely used 3-Stage Skills model systematically structures counselling theory, skills and process within a simple framework (Egan, 1986). Egan identifies the stages of counselling as exploration, new understanding and action. In the exploratory stage, the counsellor develops a warm relationship with the client thus enabling him or her to explore the problem from the client's frame of reference, before focusing on specific concerns. The skills involved are giving attention, listening and active listening. Active listening includes the counsellor's communication of empathic understanding, non-critical acceptance and genuineness, by paraphrasing, reflecting feelings, summarising, focusing and by helping the client to be specific.

In the next stage, New Understanding, the client is helped to see his or her situation in new perspectives and to focus on what might be done to cope more effectively. The client is helped to see the strengths and resources he or she might use. The counsellor's skills include giving attention and active listening, along with what Egan calls challenging skills. These comprise the communication of deeper empathic understanding (hunches, the music behind the words, educated guesses) helping the client to recognise themes, inconsistencies, behaviour patterns and feelings; giving information, including appropriate sharing of the counsellor's feelings and/or experiences; and immediacy, i.e. discussion of what is happening between counsellor and client. Preliminary goal-setting is also included in this stage, though it is covered in more depth in the third part of the process, Action.

In this final stage, the client is helped to consider possible ways to act, to look at costs and consequences, to plan action, implement it and evaluate. All the skills of stages one and two are utilised, focusing on creative thinking, problem solving and decision making, and using learning theory to plan and evaluate action. In real life, theory and practice rarely dovetail! In counselling practice the stages described above often overlap, and while the model gives an overview of the structure of the counselling process, it can at times be seen operating within the context of a single session. Nonetheless Egan's model not only describes the theory and practice of counselling, but the framework is useful in understanding other theories of counselling.

## THE COUNSELLING PROCESS

The counsellor's use of self as a therapeutic tool is fundamental to counselling theory and to the effective outcome of the counselling process. Research shows that counsellors who offer warmth, genuineness and empathy (not the same as time, sympathy and a willingness to help!) are consistently effective (Truax and Carkhuff, 1967). According to the BAC (1979), 'people become engaged in counselling when a person, occupying regularly or temporarily the role of counsellor, offers or explicitly agrees to offer time, attention and respect to another person or persons temporarily in the role of the client'. The counsellor aims to develop a therapeutic alliance with the client and to convey acceptance and understanding of the client and empathy with his or her situation. The counsellor structures the process to allow the client time and freedom to explore thoughts and feelings in an atmosphere of trust and respect. The process aims to deepen the client's understanding of his or her situation and ways of dealing with it, and thus enables choices and decisions to be based on insights gained rather than advice and directives of others (Irving and Heath, 1989).

## THE DIFFERENCE BETWEEN COUNSELLING AND THE USE OF COUNSELLING SKILLS

A large part of any GP's work is dealing with the 30 per cent of patients who present 'life problems', i.e. problems that are usually largely emotional or psychosocial. Life problems are the general practitioner's stock in trade; the problems of living and dying (Williams, 1983). Thus some of the constituent skills of counselling are needed in consultations; using open-ended and reflected questions, silence and observed inconsistencies either in what the patient says or between what the patient says and the non-verbal cues when he or she says it (Harris, 1987).

Harris hits upon a current debate in counselling circles when he argues that counselling skills are similar to clinical interviewing skills but are found in a concentrated form in nondirective counselling. This debate involves differentiating between communication skills, counselling skills and counselling. The difference between these skills has been explained in terms of the values used and the context. In essence it is this:

communication skills are discrete behaviours by which one person aims to elicit or facilitate a response in another; all people communicate with one another using basic skills such as listening, understanding, questioning, the use of silence and so on; some people are 'better' (i.e. more skilled) at communicating than others. Communication skills are value free; they are practised by a variety of people for a variety of purposes. Thus basic communication skills are used in proposing marriage, selling encyclopaedias and recommending a course of medication; it is the context in which the interaction takes place and the motivation of the communicator which contributes meaning and value. Some counsellors argue that it is only when used in a context consistent with the values of counselling that communication skills can be called counselling skills. Counselling is essentially an ethical task underpinned by a code of ethics and practice (BAC, 1989); it aims to help people identify and resolve their difficulties and live more resourcefully. It does not aim to court like the suitor, persuade like the salesperson, or advise like the doctor. While communication skills are value free, counselling skills are laden with the values of counselling (Bond, 1989).

Counselling skills, in particular the core skills of listening, reflecting and empathy, are at the heart of counselling. The counsellor uses a range of specific skills to help the client learn to manage his or her life more effectively. These skills are not the exclusive property of counsellors and are useful in many helping situations consistent with the values of counselling. Doctors, nurses, teachers and a range of professionals use such skills to facilitate their primary role. However, in the interests of clarity and good practice, it is important to stress that the use of counselling skills does not make the user a counsellor. There is a difference between using counselling skills within the confines of a surgery consultation, for example, and counselling in the formal sense outlined above. Being aware of the difference between counselling and counselling skills helps the GP to recognise when a patient might benefit from counselling and when one or two consultations in the surgery may suffice.

Whether or not the doctor should offer counselling is open to some debate (Rowland *et al.* 1989; Kelleher, 1989); while the use of counselling skills during the course of the consultation rarely leads to difficulties, more formal counselling can be far from easy and in inexperienced or untrained hands may actually cause harm (Williams, 1983). The dilemma for doctors is whether to learn to use new techniques or be content to recognise and refer (Harris, 1987). For those who appreciate the difficulties of offering and sustaining a relationship of non-possessive warmth to about two and a half thousand people for years on end (Anon., 1980) employing a practice counsellor can bring certain advantages.

## THE ROLE OF THE COUNSELLOR IN THE PRIMARY CARE TEAM

Counsellors can fulfil a number of roles within the practice team and practical examples are given in later chapters. In a survey of general practitioners working with marriage guidance counsellors (Corney, 1986), respondents felt that the counsellors' main task was counselling referred clients, but a third of the doctors mentioned that the counsellor also provided support to practice members.

### Providing support and acting as a resource for the primary care team

GPs who work with counsellors appear to value their work with patients and appreciate the opportunity to share and discuss their own feelings about patients and their relationships with them (McLeod, 1992). Employing a counsellor in the practice team seems to heighten doctors' awareness of their own reactions to patients and encourages them to improve their own counselling skills. McLeod points out that a counsellor who builds up a good relationship with a practice and who finds time for case discussion provides a new and useful resource in primary care.

The presence of the counsellor in the primary care team will thus ideally allow other professionals to see that counselling skills are a valuable part of their own expertise; district nurses, health visitors and receptionists, who make first contact with the patient, have positions which automatically place them in a counselling role. When dealing with problems, team members should be able to regard the counsellor as a colleague who shares the care-giving role and who can be approached for a different point of view, particularly when, for the patient, a referral might be seen as a rejection, and not followed up (Rowland and Hurd, 1989). Some counsellors undertake formal consultation work with GPs and other members of the team, in which there is joint discussion of the team members' relationships and work with patients; other counsellors offer training in counselling skills. Attachments have shown the benefits of the counsellor being used in this way.

## Counselling patients

Counselling aims to identify emotional problems early and to prevent more serious disturbance developing (Martin, 1988). For counselling to be successful, the presenting problem must be appropriate and meaningful and is usually of the life problem type (Williams, 1983). While there is scope for further studies aiming to identify those patients who benefit most from counselling, it appears that a wide range of problems may respond to counselling. However, those patients suffering from problems such as personality disorders, severe mental disturbance or those with psychotic tendencies usually need a different degree of help than counselling can offer. Such problems may respond better with long-term support and the use of medication, and are usually considered to be the province of the psychiatrist rather than the counsellor (Rowland, 1992).

Counsellors work with people of all ages and of all social classes, though women tend to be referred more than men (Corney, 1986). As expected in a general practice setting, the types of problems seen vary widely, although counsellors have made attempts to categorise the sort of problems they deal with. Irving and Heath (1989) categorise counselling interventions as crisis work, remedial work and developmental/educational work. Crisis work is likely to include incidents of violence, child battering, suicide attempts and sudden loss. Remedial work tends to deal with relationship problems, bereavement, sexual dysfunction, low self-esteem, low income and unemployment, anxiety and depression. Developmental work will focus on the management of stress, strengthening self-assertiveness, problems with control of teenagers and looking after elderly relatives, pre-marital counselling and behavioural problems associated with eating and smoking.

Anderson and Hasler (1979) categorise referrals into two broad camps. The first is commonly stress due to a new or crisis situation; that is often the result of marital or other relationships breaking up, bereavement, or difficulties in coping with sudden changes in personal circumstances. The second cause is stress that is the result of a long-term situation. Patients with this type of stress often have difficulty in coping with established relationships, or may not have been able to participate fully in their personal or social situations.

### The range of problems referred

The type of problem referred to the practice counsellor will depend to some extent on the availability of other resources, such as psychologists and social workers (Corney, 1986).

Waydenfeld and Waydenfeld (1980) in their study asked the participating doctors to give their reasons for referral to the counsellor. The various reasons listed showed that 42 per cent of patients were referred for anxiety, 41 per cent for marital problems, 35 per cent for another relationship problem, 14 per cent for a sexual problem, and 10 per cent for psychosomatic symptoms. Other reasons included violence, depression, alcoholism, child abuse, abortion counselling and bereavement.

Other studies of counsellor attachments document a wide range of referrals to counsellors including anxiety and stress, marital troubles and abortion (Martin and Mitchell, 1983), accommodation problems, job difficulties, depression due to unemployment, redundancy or imminent retirement, vocational guidance, financial and business problems, conflicts between generations, unsatisfied goals, and fear and loneliness in the elderly (Cohen et al., 1977). Relationship difficulties of all kinds, bereavement, alcohol-related problems, unwanted pregnancies and adolescence are also included (Corney, 1986), and Marsh and Barr (1975) list infertility, desertion, infidelity, sexual dysfunction, physical violence, alcohol-related problems, and depression among the more common presenting problems.

Given the diversity of referrals, counsellors may sometimes judge it appropriate to refer clients to agencies where more specialist help is offered. Some counsellors may also possess specialist skills, such as specific knowledge, experience and training in a special area of expertise, in addition to their basic counselling training. There are abortion counsellors, AIDS counsellors, and alcohol counsellors, to name but a few.

## Methods used

Like other members of the practice team, counsellors working in the surgery have to be generalists – that is, be able to deal with a range of problems using a variety of techniques. As many approaches to counselling are used in medical settings as elsewhere.

In a review of counselling in general practice, Wyld (1987) notes that through the skilled use of the counsellor–client relationship, counsellors aim to assist their clients to arrive at their own solution to their problems. However, the methods used by counsellors to facilitate this process are likely to differ considerably in content and style. Wyld notes the variety of techniques used in general practice, including: Rutledge's (1972) advocacy of eclecticism (a mixture of directive and non-directive techniques depending on the person and the situation involved); Harray's (1975) use of a broad range of approaches from supportive counselling to behaviour therapy; and Anderson and Hasler's (1979) use of behaviour therapy for phobias, through vocational guidance to counselling whose main aim is to offer support and insight. While counselling is essentially a non-directive listening process which avoids overt advice giving, it is not a standardised service and no two counsellors operate in the same way (Tyndall, 1985).

Some counsellors prefer to work with individuals or couples, while others may also work with families and groups. Although the majority of counselling time is spent on problem-solving work, counselling also has developmental and preventative functions and some counsellors offer sessions aiming to encourage self-awareness and self-management. Eating disorders, smoking and non-specific stress are often responsive to therapy conducted in a group or workshop setting. Group counselling can be a useful adjunct to one-to-one counselling for clients with similar or related problems, and counselling small groups of clients with like needs is often as effective as individual work (Irving and Heath, 1989).

## Length and number of sessions

Because counselling is problem-centred it is ideal for general practice. Counsellors usually allow 50 minutes per session with clients. The number of sessions offered to clients varies, partly because of the complexity of causes that bring people to counselling and partly because individual counsellors have different ways of working. Whether or not the consultation with the counsellor is precipitated by a crisis, there may be an underlying problem with long-standing antecedents which tends to require more sustained work over a longer period of time (Irving and Heath, 1989). Martin and Mitchell (1983) estimated that the counsellor saw each patient two or three times on average; in another study (Marsh and Barr, 1973) a marriage guidance counsellor saw couples for an average of 11 sessions, and Waydenfeld and Waydenfeld (1980) put the average at 15 counselling sessions. Given the throughput of patients and the undesirability of waiting lists, contracts lasting from six to ten sessions might be best suited to general practice, rather than long-term intensive therapy. Patients who need more than counsellors can offer within the confines of general practice are usually referred to an outside agency, such as the local mental health team for clinical psychology treatment, or to a private psychotherapy service.

## SUMMARY

Counselling is more than a shoulder to cry on. Counsellors aim to help people come to terms with their difficulties and identify ways of coping more effectively and resourcefully. Although there are many theories of counselling, in essence counselling is an ethical task in which the counsellor forms a therapeutic alliance with the client and uses a range of skills to facilitate the client's resolution of his or her problems. There is a difference between counselling in the formal sense described in this chapter and the use of counselling skills.

Although there is scope for further research into the effectiveness of counselling, GPs who employ counsellors find that short-term counselling is often appropriate for patients presenting 'life problems'. Practice counsellors may work with individuals, couples or groups, using a variety of techniques to address the wide range of problems referred. Finally, a practice counsellor can be a resource to the doctors and other members of the primary care team facilitating joint discussion of their relationships with patients and encouraging the development of their counselling skills.

## REFERENCES

Anderson, S. A. and Hasler, J. C. (1979) 'Counselling in general practice', *Journal of the Royal College of General Practitioners* 29: 352–6.

Anon. (1980) 'Is counselling the key?', *Journal of the Royal College of General Practitioners* 30: 643–5.

Bond, T. (1989) 'Towards defining the role of counselling skills', *Counselling* 69: 3–9.

BAC (1979) *Counselling: Definition of Terms in Use with Expansion and Rationale*, Rugby: British Association for Counselling.

BAC (1989) *Code of Ethics and Practice for Counsellors*, Rugby: British Association for Counselling.

BAC (1992) *Invitation to Membership*, Rugby: British Association for Counselling.

Cohen, J. and Halpern, A. (1978) 'A practice counsellor', *Journal of the Royal College of General Practitioners* 20: 481–4.

Cohen, J. S. H., Dominian, J. and Woodhouse, D. (1977) *Proceedings of the Royal Society of Medicine* 70: 495–502.

Combs, A. W. (1989) *A Theory of Therapy: Guidelines for Counselling Practice*, Newbury Park: Sage.

Corney, R. (1986) 'Marriage guidance counselling in general practice', *Journal of the Royal College of General Practitioners* 36: 424–6.

Egan, A. S. (1986) *The Skilled Helper*, USA: Brooks/Cole (3rd edn).

Harray, A. S. (1975) 'The role of a counsellor in a medical centre', *New Zealand Medical Journal* 82: 383–5

Harris, C. M. (1987) 'Let's do away with counselling' in D.J.P. Gray (ed.), *Medical Annual*, Bristol: Wright, pp. 105–11.

Herink, R. (1980) *The Psychotherapy Handbook: the A–Z Guide to More than 250 Therapies in Use Today*, New York: Meridian Books.

Irving, J. and Heath, V. (1989) *Counselling in General Practice: a Guide for General Practitioners* (revised edn), Rugby: British Association for Counselling.

Kelleher, D. (1989) 'The general practitioner as counsellor: an examination of counselling by general practitioners', *Counselling Psychology Review* 4: 7–13.

Knight, L. (1986) *Talking to a Stranger: A Consumer's Guide to Therapy*, London: Fontana.

McLeod, J. (1992) 'Counselling in primary health care, the GP's perspective', in M. Sheldon (ed.), *Royal College of General Practitioners Clinical Series on Counselling in General Practice*, London: RCGP Enterprises.

Marsh, G. N. and Barr, J. (1975) 'Marriage guidance counselling in a group practice', *Journal of the Royal College of General Practitioners* 25: 73–5.

Martin, E. (1988) 'Counsellors in general practice; evidence of benefit needed before widespread adoption', *British Medical Journal* 297: 637.

Martin, E. and Mitchell, H. (1983) 'A counsellor in general practice: a one year survey', *Journal of the Royal College of General Practitioners* 33: 366–7.

Munro, E. A. Manthei, R. J. and Small, J. J. (1983) *Counselling: A Skills Approach* (revised edn), New Zealand: Methuen.

Rowland, N. (1992) 'Counselling and counselling skills', in M. Sheldon (ed.), *Royal College of General Practitioners Clinical Series on Counselling in General Practice*, London: RCGP.

Rowland, N. and Hurd, J. (1989) *Counselling in General Practice: A Guide for Counsellors* (revised edn), Rugby: British Association for Counselling.

Rowland, N. Irving J. and Maynard, A. K. (1989) 'Can GPs counsel?', *Journal of the Royal College of General Practitioners* 39: 118–20.

Rutledge, M. (1972) 'Counselling in general practice', *Australian Family Physician* 29: 461–4.

Sutton, C. (1987) 'The evaluation of counselling; a goal attainment approach', *Counselling*, 60: 14–20.

Truax, C. B. and Carkhuff, R. R. (1967) *Towards Effective Counselling and Psychotherapy Training and Practice*, Chicago: Aldine.

Tyndall, N. (1985) 'The work and impact of the National Marriage Guidance Council' in W. Dryden (ed.), *Marital Therapy in Britain*, Vol. 1, London: Harper and Row.

Waydenfeld, D. and Waydenfeld, S. (1980) 'Counselling in general practice', *Journal of the Royal College of General Practitioners* 30: 671–7.

Williams, I. (1983) 'The counselling approach in general practice', *Update* 1815–23.

Wyld, K. L. (1987) 'Counselling in general practice; a review', *British Journal of Guidance and Counselling* 9: 129–41.

# Chapter 4

# Studies of the effectiveness of counselling in general practice

*Roslyn Corney*

## THE NEED FOR EVALUATION

Many counsellors and doctors question the need for the evaluation of counselling. indicating that they know that it works because their clients tell them so. Indeed, studies of consumer opinion almost universally suggest that clients find counselling helpful. There is also the widely held belief that counselling is beneficial and should be available to the troubled and distressed. However, there are a number of reasons why evaluative studies are so essential.

First, preliminary studies suggest that some patients may be helped more than others. In a time of limited resources, it is essential to focus on those individuals who can benefit most from counselling. Evaluative studies should identify these patients.

Secondly, it is a common finding that there is greater variance in outcome in treated clients than in untreated controls, suggesting that some individuals may possibly be harmed by therapy. Evaluative trials should aim to identify those patients who may be harmed.

Thirdly, there are a wide range of therapies ranging from behavioural approaches to psychoanalysis. We urgently need to know the therapies that benefit patients most and the ones that are more acceptable to patients.

Fourthly, in terms of training and considerations of manpower, it is important to know the level of skills that is necessary for benefit to occur. How much training and what level of expertise is necessary for benefit to occur? This is linked to all three prior questions. Some clients may benefit most by the setting up of a self-help group, while the more seriously disturbed/

damaged client will probably need skilful and knowledgeable handling.

This chapter will consider the evidence of the value of placing counsellors in general practice, including the results of surveys, consumer opinions and clinical trials.

## SUBJECTIVE ACCOUNTS

Subjective accounts suggest that the attachment of counsellors works well, with much consumer, counsellor and GP satisfaction. One study conducted by the Waydenfelds found that 44 of the 47 clients who completed a client questionnaire indicated that help was received (Waydenfeld and Waydenfeld, 1980). This same study investigated the outcome of 25 patients who had previously been referred to the psychiatrist and were now referred to the counsellor. They found that 20 patients were considered by the doctor and/or the counsellor to have been either greatly or somewhat improved by counselling, four were considered not to have improved, and one was considered to be worse.

Another study by Anderson and Hasler (1979) sent questionnaires to the first 80 patients referred to the counsellor. Fifty-five patients returned them (69 per cent). Of this group, 47 agreed that counselling should be available in general practice, 43 would use the counselling service again and 46 would recommend it to their relatives or friends. The clients also considered that they had been helped considerably, as can be seen from Table 4.1.

## UTILISATION OF MEDICAL SERVICES

Other studies have considered whether counselling has had any effect on the utilisation of medical services. The results have been used as a measure of outcome (for example, if the client makes fewer visits to the doctor or stops taking psychotropic drugs, he or she is assumed to be well or better). Many studies have indeed shown a reduction in visits made to the doctor (Marsh and Barr, 1975; Waydenfeld and Waydenfeld, 1980) after cessation of counselling in contrast with a period before. A similar number of studies have found a reduction in the number of psychotropic and other drugs prescribed (Cohen, 1977; Meacher, 1977; Waydenfeld and Waydenfeld, 1980). Other studies have indicated that there was a reduction in referrals to psychiatrists

*Table 4.1*  The views of 55 patients on how they had been helped by counselling

|  | Yes | No | No answer |
|---|---|---|---|
| Has there been any improvement in the way you feel about yourself? | 35 | 19 | 1 |
| Has there been any improvement in your close personal relationships? | 26 | 27 | 2 |
| Has there been any improvement in your contacts with friends? | 25 | 25 | 5 |
| Has there been a change in the way you feel about your past experiences? | 22 | 30 | 3 |
| Has there been a change in the way you feel about your personal situation? | 38 | 15 | 2 |
| Do you feel more capable of dealing with your change of mood? | 39 | 13 | 3 |
| Do you feel more self-confident? | 27 | 25 | 3 |

after a counselling attachment had been instigated (Illman, 1983; Corney, 1987a).

However, the reduction in medical utilisation rates has also been used to argue a case for the cost-effectiveness of counselling. Consideration needs to be given, however, on whether we should try to argue the case for attaching counsellors in general practice in terms of cost-effectiveness. A successful attachment of a counsellor may result in more time being spent in discussing cases with other members of the primary care team. It may also result in the primary care professionals spending more time in their consultations with patients as they start to adopt a more caring patient-centred approach. While this change in approach may have far-reaching consequences in terms of comprehensive care, the effects may be extremely difficult to trace and cost.

An attempt was made in a study carried out by Martin and Martin (1985) to investigate whether having a counsellor in the practice had altered GP behaviour. The notes of 300 patients who had been continuously registered with the practice since 1974 were randomly withdrawn from the files. The number of psychosocial problems and the number of prescriptions for psychotropic drugs recorded in the years 1975, 1979 and 1982 were noted. They found that the number of patients who had had a psychiatric diagnosis recorded in their notes during one year fell between 1975 and 1982, the number of prescriptions for anti-depressant drugs fell (17 per cent decrease) but the prescriptions for tranquillisers and sleeping tablets rose (30 per cent increase). They hypothesised that the change in psychotropic prescriptions could have been due to the doctor becoming more willing to consider psychogenic problems as being precipitated by stress rather than a biochemical change. The reduction in patients being given a psychiatric diagnosis could be due to early attention to patients' emotional needs, preventing later breakdowns. The authors conclude, however, that no major changes were detected over the seven-year period.

These authors also carried out a second survey comparing the outcome of a group of 87 patients receiving counselling with a matched group of patients drawn from the age–sex register. They found no major differences in outcome between the two groups, although this was only measured in terms of attendance rate and psychotropic drug prescription. As the controls were only matched according to their age and sex and not their social/psychological characteristics, it is difficult to draw conclusions from the results.

## CLINICAL TRIALS UNDERTAKEN

In medicine, clinical trials are normally undertaken in order to evaluate whether a treatment works or not. In clinical trials, the progress of one group of patients who receive the treatment is compared with the progress of patients who do not. However, clinical trials are extremely difficult to undertake and most studies evaluating counselling are flawed in some way – some more than others. It must be remembered that we are at an early stage in refining our techniques of evaluation. It is important to be aware of some of the difficulties and value judgements involved so that we evaluate the merits of the studies as well as be aware of the results.

Some of the problems encountered are outlined in Chapter 9. These include: difficulties in deciding who is the client group; what is improvement and how to measure and assess it; when to carry out follow-up assessments; how to assess the treatment, the quality of the therapist, the client motivation and the relationship developed between client and therapist.

Ideally, any study should also evaluate the other effects of having a counsellor based in the practice in addition to changes in the actual patients referred. For example, a counsellor may increase the sensitivity of other team members to psychological problems and help them feel more confident in managing some of these problems.

The chapter does not include all the clinical trials of therapy undertaken in general practice. The trials investigating counsellors are included as well as some of the trials of other professions who take on a counselling/psychotherapeutic role in general practice. This includes nurses, psychologists and social workers.

## CLINICAL TRIALS OF COUNSELLORS

The first clinical trial conducted was carried out by Ashurst and colleagues. In this study, 726 patients aged between 16 and 65 from a health centre and a group practice were randomly assigned to counselling or to routine GP treatment (Ashurst and Ward, 1983). Patients were referred to the study if they had consulted their GP for a neurotic disorder. High proportions had been prescribed psychotropic drugs. The two counsellors generally favoured a non-directive approach, making use of progressive relaxation, supportive counselling, interpretative psychotherapy, transactional analysis, behavioural techniques, Gestalt and dream work.

While a high proportion of the patients valued the help they had received, no striking differences in outcome (measured one year later) between groups were elicited, although it was felt by the authors that some individuals benefited considerably. One of the problems with this pioneering study was the question of client motivation. Not all the patients recruited into the study specifically wanted counselling help, and this is likely to have reduced the effects of treatment.

The second study, carried out in Sydney, Australia, compared the outcome of three groups to which patients had been randomly assigned (Brodaty and Andrews, 1983). Patients were again aged between 18 and 65 and had had persistent psychological symptoms for at least six months. In one group, 18 patients received eight weekly half-hour sessions of brief problem-oriented dynamic psychotherapy from a trained psychotherapist. Another group of 18 individuals received eight weekly half-hour appointments with their family doctor (who had no specific training). The third group of 20 patients received no additional therapy. No differences were found between three treatment groups in outcome scores measuring symptom severity, social dysfunction, physical disability or medication.

The third study was recently conducted by Stanton and Corney on patients with marital problems. Analysis of the results is still progressing and has not yet been published. Depressed women with marital difficulties have been found to have the poorest prognosis without outside help (Corney, 1987b). In addition, men and women with marital problems are more likely to seek help from their doctor than from any other agency.

In this study four counsellors were attached to six general practices specifically for the purposes of the study. The counsellors were all trained and accredited but were not all trained by Relate. These practices were all situated in inner southeast London, a deprived area of mixed racial composition where many patients have multiple social problems. GPs were asked to refer men and women with 'marital' problems. They had to be still living together at the time of referral (but not necessarily married) and to have been together for at least one year. These criteria were used as it is wise in clinical trials to concentrate on a homogeneous group. It was also felt that the limited counselling resources available were best focused on helping those relationships where there had been some commitment to staying together.

Subjects were given an initial psychiatric, social and marital assessment and medical utilisation data for the previous six months obtained from the notes. Subjects were then randomly allocated to one group who received counselling help or to the waiting list control group who were offered counselling after the follow-up assessment at six months. Subjects were also reassessed twelve months after referral.

Because of problems in obtaining suitable subjects (because of the entry criteria), only 47 subjects were included in the trial. Approximately 80 per cent of subjects referred were female and their mean age was the late 30s. Three-quarters were of European origin and three-quarters had had marital problems for over one year.

At six months, those referred to the counsellor had made much more improvement than the controls. There were statistically significant differences between groups in their scores measuring depression, self-esteem, and in some of the ratings measuring marital adjustment. Although other measures of outcome were not statistically significant – for example, medical utilisation data – the counselled group tended to show more improvement on these than the waiting list controls. Analysis of the twelve-month assessment is not yet available.

## OTHER STUDIES OF COUNSELLING METHODS USED BY OTHER PROFESSIONS

### Health visitors

One recent study has been conducted to evaluate the effectiveness of health visitors in counselling women with postnatal depression (Holden *et al.*, 1989). The health visitor is in the best position to identify postnatal depression with one of her major responsibilities being the care of the newborn. In this study, health visitors were given training in Rogerian counselling. They were given a manual describing postnatal depression and non-directive counselling and attended three weekly training sessions of two hours. These group training sessions made use of videotapes and included instruction in counselling methods such as non-verbal encouragement and reflection. Significant psychiatric improvement (assessed by psychiatric interview and self-assessments) was obtained at three months in the group seen by the specially trained health visitors for eight weekly visits in comparison with the controls.

### Community psychiatric nurses

In recent years, there has been a rapid, largely uncharted, development of community psychiatric nursing. In 1985, there were 3,000 community psychiatric nurses (CPNs) in the United Kingdom; the projections are for 4,500 in 1990 and 7,500 for 1995 (CPNA, 1985). General practitioners are the largest group referring patients to CPNs. These patients include those with psychotic, neurotic and other mood disorders.

In one trial, CPNs working in the community were compared with routine outpatient psychiatric treatment and patients were followed up every six months for over 18 months (Paykel *et al.*,

1982). No differences were found between effectiveness of the two modes of service on symptoms, social adjustment or family burden, suggesting that the two treatments were comparable in terms of outcome. However, patients seeing CPNs reported greater satisfaction with treatment. Community psychiatric nursing resulted in an appreciable reduction in patients' contacts with psychiatrists and other staff, more discharges, and only a small increase in contact with general practitioners for prescriptions.

In another study (Mangen et al., 1983; Marks, 1985), nurse therapists were used. These psychiatric nurses were especially trained to undertake behavioural psychotherapy. The findings indicated that neurotic patients (including those with phobias, habit disorders, sexual dysfunctioning and obsessive-compulsive disorders) had a better outcome post-treatment at one year after receiving behavioural psychotherapy than after routine treatment from a general practitioner. In addition, the controls who had not improved after one year were given the option of receiving behavioural treatment. After the treatment, they made significant improvement while no gains were made in the drop-outs or in those who refused treatment. Cost–benefit analyses suggest that benefits, in terms of reduced time off work and less use of health resources, outweighed the costs of employing the therapists.

### Clinical psychologists

In 1977, it was estimated that approximately 14 per cent of clinical psychologists work with GPs (Broadhurst, 1977) and it is likely that these figures have increased. General practitioners refer to clinical psychologists patients with a wide range of difficulties, including anxiety, phobias, depression, psychosomatic conditions and habit disorders. Patients show a high degree of satisfaction with behavioural treatment, and, as with other professionals, studies have shown reduced psychotropic drug prescriptions and fewer consultations (Ives, 1979; Koch, 1979; Trepka et al., 1986), although these effects may not be long-lasting (Freeman and Button, 1984).

However, the evidence of more sophisticated studies with control groups is more conflicting with many studies only showing short-term effects. In a study conducted by Robson et al. (1984), assessments were made initially and at 14, 22, 34 and 52 weeks after commencement of treatment. Patients referred to a psychologist improved more quickly on scales measuring psychosocial changes; they made fewer visits to the doctor and received fewer psychotropic drug prescriptions. At one year, however, there were no major differences between groups because of the continued improvement of the control patients. The reduction in the number of visits to the doctor was more pronounced in the interpersonal and habit disorder subgroups and less noticeable for depressed and anxious patients. The authors estimated that 28 per cent of the clinical psychologists' salaries could be found from drug economies alone.

The studies carried out by Teasdale and co-authors (1984) show similar results, with patients receiving treatment improving more quickly but with few differences at later follow-up assessments due to continued improvement of the controls. Earll and Kincey (1982) found no differences between groups at seven months in the majority of ratings used, including GP consultation rates. However, patients receiving psychological treatment had reduced psychotropic drug prescriptions during the treatment period and were very satisfied with the treatment received.

## Social workers

The first study conducted on social workers in primary care attachments found significant differences in outcome between a group of chronic neurotics who had been referred to a special experimental service (which included a social worker) than a control group of patients (selected from a number of different practices) receiving routine care from their GP (Cooper *et al.*, 1975). At the end of one year, the experimental group made more improvement socially and clinically, had received fewer prescriptions of psychotropic drugs and were considered by their GP to need less medical care.

In a later study, women suffering from acute or acute on chronic depression were either allocated to a social worker attached to a general practice or referred for routine treatment (Corney, 1984). Overall, there was no additional benefit from the social work treatment at six months and one year follow-up, except for one group. These were women with acute on chronic depression who also had poor relationships with their spouses or boyfriends. Many also had poor social contacts and tended to be isolated. Analysis of the records of the social workers also showed that this group were the most highly motivated to receive help. These findings indicate the importance of conducting 'within group' analyses.

The social workers in both these studies gave much practical help as well as counselling, such as arranging day nursery placements, accommodation, claiming benefits, etc. The results of both these studies suggest that practical help as well as emotional support is beneficial. Indeed, studies of clients' views reinforce this finding (Mayer and Timms, 1970).

In the third study – a cross-over trial – depressed patients were allocated to individual cognitive therapy, group cognitive therapy, or a waiting list control group. Those who had cognitive therapy from a social worker did significantly better at three months than those on the waiting list. There was no significant difference in outcome between patients treated with group or individual cognitive therapy. Unfortunately, no longer-term assessment was possible because the study was a cross-over trial (Ross and Scott, 1985).

**The GP as counsellor**

One area which has not been extensively researched is evaluating the effectiveness of the GP as counsellor. In one study by Catalan and colleagues (1984), patients were randomly assigned to one group who received a prescription for anxiolytics or to another group who were given brief counselling by the GPs and no prescription. Improvement at one and seven months were similar in both groups, suggesting that brief counselling was as effective as drugs. The authors suggest that such counselling need not be intensive or specially skilled and concluded that anxiety may often be reduced to tolerable levels by means of explanation, exploration of feelings, reassurance and encouragement.

In another study the use of stress self-help packages administered by the GP was compared with routine GP treatment (Kiely and McPherson, 1986). Patients were included in the study if they had psychological problems that were potentially stress related. The authors found greater improvement at three months in those receiving the package, and this group also visited the GP less often for psychological problems.

It has been argued that GPs find it difficult to take on the role of counsellor (Rowland *et al.*, 1989). The GP is normally directive and practical, prescribing treatment – and patients come to expect this. However, some patients find it difficult to accept referral elsewhere, wanting to be helped by someone they know and trust. The major problem is that GPs have little time available for longer sessions. However, even if GPs do offer some form of counselling to their patients, there will still be patients needing more time and expertise who would benefit from referral elsewhere.

## META ANALYSIS

A meta analysis of eleven British studies of specialist mental health treatment in general practice was undertaken by Balestrieri and colleagues in 1988. In each study the outcome of treatment by a specialist mental health professional located in general practice was compared with the outcome of the usual treatment given by general practitioners. The main finding was that treatment by mental health professionals was about 10 per cent more successful than that usually given by general practitioners. Counselling, behaviour therapy, and general psychiatry proved to be similar in their overall effect. The influence of counselling seemed to be greatest on social functioning, whereas behaviour therapy seemed mainly to reduce contacts with the psychiatric services.

## CONCLUSIONS

The results of these studies give tentative support of the value of counselling in general practice. The more recent studies have tended to yield more positive results. It is important for the investigator to consider the difficult problem of client motivation: if subjects are included in trials with poor motivation, then we are not conducting a fair trial of counselling. The later studies tend to be more specific in their entry criteria.

The study conducted using health visitors who received minimal counselling training suggests that counsellors should not be too élitist in suggesting that only they can conduct counselling in general practice. Ashurst, in her study, recorded a suspicion that the method employed by the counsellor was far less important than the relationship which developed between counsellor and client. The counselling roles of all existing professionals in primary care – health visitors, GPs, practice nurses and others – should be considered and attention should be paid to developing their skills. A counsellor in a practice can perhaps do this by initiating case discussion with other members of the team or by conducting joint interviews. Training other professions does not preclude the role of more highly trained professionals who can be called upon to counsel the more difficult cases. A skilled counsellor can only see a few clients each week; the mass of problems seen in primary care, particularly in deprived areas, indicates the urgent need to train and develop the skills of all workers in this setting.

## REFERENCES

Anderson, S. and Hasler, J. (1979) 'Counselling in general practice', *Journal of the Royal College of General Practitioners* 29: 352–6.

Ashurst, P. M. and Ward, D. F. (1983) *An Evaluation of Counselling in General Practice*, Final report of the Leverhulme Counselling Project. Report available from the Mental Health Foundation, London.

Balestrieri, M., Williams, P. and Wilkinson, G. (1988) 'Specialist mental health treatment in general practice: a meta-analysis', *Psychological Medicine* 18: 711–17.

Broadhurst, A. (1977) 'What part does general practice play in community clinical psychology?', *Bulletin of the British Psychological Society* 30: 304–9.

Brodaty, H. and Andrews, G. (1983) 'Brief psychotherapy in family practice. A controlled prospective intervention trial', *British Journal of Psychiatry* 143: 11–19.

Catalan, J., Gath, D., Edmonds, G. and Ennis, J. (1984) 'The effects of non-prescribing of Anxiolytics in general practice. I. Controlled evaluation of psychiatric and social outcome', *British Journal of Psychiatry* 144: 603–10.

Cohen, J. S. H. (1977) 'Marital counselling in general practice', *Proceedings of the Royal College of Medicine* 70: 495–6.

CPNA (1985) *The 1985 CPNA National Survey Update*, Bristol: Community Psychiatric Nurses Association.

Cooper, B., Harwin, B. J., Delpa, C. and Shepherd, M. (1975) 'Mental health care in the community: an evaluative study', *Psychological Medicine* 5: 372–80.

Corney, R. (1984) 'The effectiveness of attached social workers in the management of depressed female patients in general practice', *Psychological Medicine* 14 (monograph suppl. 6): 47.

Corney, R. (1987a) 'Marriage guidance counselling in general practice in London', *British Journal of Guidance and Counselling* 15: 50–8.

Corney, R. H. (1987b) 'Marital problems and treatment outcome in depressed women', *British Journal of Psychiatry* 151: 652–9.

Earll, L. and Kincey, J. (1982) 'Clinical psychology in general practice', *Journal of the Royal College of General Practitioners* 32: 32–7.

Freeman, G. K. and Button, E. J. (1984) 'The clinical psychologist in general practice: a six-year study of consulting patterns for psychosocial problems', *Journal of the Royal College of General Practitioners* 34: 337-80.

Holden, J. M., Sagovsky, R. and Cox, J. L. (1989) 'Counselling in a general practice setting: controlled study of health visitor intervention in treatment of postnatal depression', *British Medical Journal* 298: 223–6.

Illman, J. (1983) 'Is psychiatric referral good value for money?', *BMA New Review* 9: 41–2.

Ives, G. (1979) 'Psychological treatment in general practice', *Journal of the Royal College of General Practitioners* 29: 343–51.

Kiely, B. G. and McPherson, I. G. (1986) 'Stress self-help packages in primary care: a controlled trial evaluation', *Journal of the Royal College of General Practitioners* 36: 307–9.

Koch, H. C. H. (1979) 'Evaluation of behaviour therapy intervention in general practice', *Journal of the Royal College of General Practitioners* 29: 337–40.

Mangen, S. P., Paykel, E. S., Griffith, J. H. *et al.* (1983) 'Cost-effectiveness of community psychiatric nurse or outpatient psychiatrist care of neurotic patients', *Psychological Medicine* 13: 407–16.

Marks, I. (1985) 'Controlled trial of psychiatric nurse therapists in primary care', *British Medical Journal* 290: 1181–4.

Marsh, G. N. and Barr, J. (1975) 'Marriage guidance counselling in a group practice', *Journal of the Royal College of General Practitioners* 25: 73–5.

Martin, E. and Martin, P. M. L. (1985) 'Changes in psychological diagnosis and prescription in a practice employing a counsellor', *Family Practice* 2: 241–3.

Mayer, J. E. and Timms, N. (1970) *The Client Speaks*, London: Routledge & Kegan Paul.

Meacher, M. (1977) *A Pilot Counselling Scheme with General Practitioners: Summary Report*, London: Mental Health Foundation (unpublished).

Paykel, E. S., Mangen, S. P., Griffith, J. H. and Burns, T. P. (1982) 'Community psychiatric nursing for neurotic patients: a controlled study', *British Journal of Psychiatry* 140: 573–81.

Robson, M. H., France, R. and Bland, M. (1984) 'Clinical psychologists in primary care: controlled clinical and economic evaluation', *British Medical Journal* 288: 1805–8.

Ross, M. and Scott, M. (1985) 'An evaluation of the effectiveness of individual and group cognitive therapy in the treatment of depressed patients in an inner city health centre', *Journal of the Royal College of General Practitioners* 35: 239–42.

Rowland, N., Irving, J. and Maynard, A. (1989) 'Can general practitioners counsel?', *Journal of the Royal College of General Practitioners* 39: 118–20.

Teasdale, J. D., Fennell, M. J. V., Hibbert, G.A. *et al.* (1984) 'Cognitive therapy for major depressive disorder in primary care', *British Journal of Psychiatry* 144: 400–6.

Trepka, C., Laing, I. and Smith, S. (1986) 'Group treatment of general practice anxiety problems', *Journal of the Royal College of General Practitioners* 36: 114–17.

Waydenfeld, D. and Waydenfeld, S. W. (1980) 'Counselling in general practice', *Journal of the Royal College of General Practitioners* 30: 671–7.

# Chapter 5

# The ethics of counselling

*Rachel Jenkins and Raanan Gillon*

Why is it important to consider the ethics of counselling? Surely if therapists are people of good character, conscience and integrity, that is enough? Of course good character, conscience and integrity are necessary virtues; however, as we hope to make clear, they are not sufficient in themselves to deal with the conflicts that can arise in any counsellor's practice.

Conscience is an ambiguous concept. The *Oxford English Dictionary* defines it both as an 'internal conviction . . . the faculty or principle which pronounces upon the moral quality of one's actions or motives, approving the right and condemning the wrong' and as 'inward knowledge . . . inmost thought . . . internal recognition of the moral quality of one's motives and actions'. Thus it is a concept of an unthinking but morally controlling force or it is a concept of an essentially rational faculty – being able to reflect intelligently on moral matters (Hughes, 1980) – 'a mode of thought about one's acts and their rightness or wrongness, goodness and badness' (Beauchamp and Childress, 1983).

It is therefore obvious that in order to assess whether the claim that good conscience is all that is required for the ethics of counselling, we need to know which of these two concepts of conscience is intended. If the non-thinking, non-rational faculty of conscience is intended, the problem of conflict of conscience, whether intrapersonal or interpersonal, is left unamenable to reason. For example, if counsellor A decides to alert the GP that a patient is suicidal, regardless of the patient's own desires, and counsellor B decides not to alert the GP about such a patient, where stands the ethics of counselling? Which position is right and why? Are both right? Why is no resolution or even attempt at resolution possible or desirable?

The obvious way out of such an impasse is to choose the second concept of conscience, in which the exercise of reason is an essential element; but if that concept of conscience is chosen, the original view – that moral philosophy can be dispensed with and that ethics of counselling can be allowed to rest on conscience, good character and integrity – becomes empty, because 'making reasoned judgements about moral questions' and 'thought about one's acts and their rightness or wrongness' are the main constituents of the activity of moral philosophy.

Integrity is also an ambiguous concept. It can mean some morally specified and admirable condition such as 'sinlessness . . . soundness of moral principle . . . uprightness, honesty, sincerity' or it can mean completeness or wholeness. The usual meaning of integrity in moral philosophy relies on the second, more literal, concept of moral wholeness or of being one's own person. It requires identifying oneself with a particular moral stance and sticking to it in the face of temptation to abandon it; it also entails a sense of what one can and cannot live with, and is thus a fundamental part of one's moral character and identity. This sense of integrity, however, does not obviate the need for moral criticism, reflection and argument any more than does reliance on one's (unreflective) conscience.

Can reliance in good or virtuous character (in association with good conscience and integrity) be sufficient for the ethics of counselling and obviate the need for philosophical ethics? Not unless we agree what the virtues of a good counsellor are. This is a widely debated question, and critical assessment of the different viewpoints is essential.

## THE FOUR PRINCIPLES

Beauchamp and Childress (1983) have outlined four prima facie principles of ethics which, they argue, cut across all ethical, moral and political perspectives, and these are:

1. The principle of autonomy
2. The principle of beneficence
3. The principle of non maleficence
4. The principle of justice.

Each of these will be discussed, in turn, in relation to counselling.

## The principle of autonomy

Autonomy (literally, self-rule) is the capacity to think, decide and act on the basis of such thought, and do so freely and independently. It is not simply doing what one wants to do, but is doing what one wants to do on the basis of thought or reason. Thus the concept of autonomy incorporates the exercise of rationality, and it can be applied to thoughts (making decisions, believing things, having aesthetic preferences and making moral assessments), intentions, will power (willing that one shall do something) and actions (doing things).

In respect for autonomy we are concerned with the autonomy of all affected by a proposed action. We are not just concerned here with autonomy of oneself, but also with respect for other people's autonomy. But people's autonomous intentions may conflict, and this raises immediate questions for psychiatry, psychotherapy and counselling. For example, how far should the therapist decide what is good for the patient? How far has the therapist a right to decide or diagnose what is disordered in the patient or client, and how far should the client concerned decide? This is a major issue which touches on respect for personal autonomy, but it is clearly complicated by psychiatric and psychological theories suggesting that the client is often not able to perceive what is wrong.

This argument is reminiscent of other areas of medical practice where the experts also know better – or think they know better – than the client. In such circumstances, it is often revealing to work out what one's own view would be when the therapist of any sort – doctor, psychotherapist, or whatever – decides that he or she knows better than you what is good for you, what is bad for you, what is wrong with you and what is right for you. The issue is not about whether there are expert areas of knowledge, rather it is about the principle that such knowledge should be given to the client to enable the client to decide what to do about it. If the client decides to reject the expert advice, should the therapist agree with the client, or try to persuade the client to adopt the expert view, or absolutely override the client?

Two further aspects of the principle of respect for autonomy are the question of confidentiality and the question of how much to tell the patient or client. How much to tell the patient has already been referred to in the previous paragraph, but needs further exploration. When patients ask for an explanation of their symptoms, or perhaps even when they do not ask, how much are you actually going to explain to them about the nature of what is happening, and (as will be discussed in the next section) how much are you going to explain the probabilities of different kinds of benefits and harms.

On the question of confidentiality, is psychotherapy a strictly confidential activity? Is it something that is so absolutely confidential that in no circumstances should confidentiality be overridden? One of the characteristics of the four principles approach outlined above is that none of these principles is absolute. It is not possible for them to be so because in a situation where they conflict with each other, one or another will have to prevail. If one of them were absolute, then the other areas would no longer be independent principles.

The same lack of absoluteness applies to confidentiality in the context of psychotherapy. A good example which raises some of the issues involved is the famous Tarasoff case, in America, where a client told his psychotherapist that he was going to kill his ex-girlfriend when she came back from Brazil. The psychotherapist told his superior and gave his view that the client should be compulsorily admitted to hospital, but for various reasons this did not happen, and the client did indeed subsequently kill the girlfriend, as he had said he would do. At the ensuing court case there was a split judgement, two to one in favour of the view that the client should have been hospitalised and the victim and her parents warned.

It is important to work out for oneself what one would do in similar circumstances, and for the professional organisations concerned to consider their own stances. Clearly the principle of respect for the autonomy of all affected does not require absolute confidentiality.

Kant argued that one must always 'act in such a way that you treat humanity, whether in your own person or in the person of any other, never simply as a means but always at the same time as an end'. For Kant, respect for autonomy was a logically necessary feature of being a rational agent, and he argued that respect for the autonomy of any individual human being could be exercised only within the context of respect for the autonomy of all other (autonomous) human beings (Kant: see Paton, 1974). Mill also argued for the moral obligation to respect people's autonomy, supporting this claim on the utilisation grounds that such respect would maximise human welfare (Mill: see Warnock, 1974).

An obvious counterclaim to this stance is that, although respect for autonomy may be important, it is often more important to do the best for people, and especially one's patients – or at least to minimise the harm they suffer. To do this it may be necessary to override their wishes and to treat them merely as means to an end, that is, as a means to their own recovery. This argument has been well rehearsed in relation to medicine, but may also be applied to any therapy, including counselling. However, even if one accepts the claim that the overriding moral requirement is to do one's best to improve the health of patients, to minimise their suffering and prolong their lives, it is by no means clear that these ends are furthered by, for example, false confidence, paternalistic decision making, evasions, deceit or even downright lies.

A second counterclaim is that doctors, therapists and counsellors may indeed have more expert knowledge than the patient or client. This is, of course, likely to be true in the technical sphere, but it does not follow that the doctor or counsellor is better trained than the client to make moral assessments. Even if that were true, many would object on the grounds that it is not the doctor's or the counsellor's role even to advise on a patient's moral decisions, let alone make them.

## The principle of beneficence

Beneficence (the central obligation to benefit people: especially, in this context, our patients or clients) and non-maleficence (with minimal harm) are really two quite separate principles, but when one is trying to help people to benefit, then it is necessary to regard them together, because when one tries to help someone, one always risks harming that person, and so one always risks maleficence. The overall objective in any sort of medical or health care is to produce a net benefit over harm rather than avoid harm at all costs. The duty to produce net benefit over harm may also be called the duty of care (though this term is sometimes used in relation to the strictly legal duty of care). More research is needed into whether counselling actually does benefit patients/clients and, furthermore, into the kind of counselling that benefits them most, with the least expenditure of resources (see Chapter 4). (This is also important in the context of the last of the four principles.) Furthermore, there is a major role for clinical audit in establishing whether patients are routinely being benefited with minimal harm.

First of all, of course, we need to discuss what constitutes benefiting and harming them. Even in this context there is a need to respect autonomy, since, for many people, simply respecting their autonomy constitutes benefiting them, and overriding their autonomy constitutes harming them. Those therapists who do not ask clients what they themselves see as beneficial and harmful, and who do not accommodate and integrate the clients' views about those matters, are in fact not only overriding autonomy but are also more likely to be harmful than beneficial.

Three important constraints to beneficence include

(1) the need to respect the autonomy of those whom one intends to help, especially to find out what it is they want in the way of help (the duty of beneficence needs to be tempered by the duty of respect for autonomy);
(2) the need to ensure that the help one renders is not bought at too high a price (the duty of beneficence needs to be tempered by the duty of non-maleficence);
(3) the need to consider the wants, needs and rights of others (the duty of beneficence must be tempered by the duty of justice).

### Duty of respect for autonomy

If one wants to do good for a client, one generally needs to find out what he or she actually wants to do. Sometimes this may not need much enquiry, but often, in even the simplest of interactions, different clients in similar circumstances may want different things from their counsellors. One client, after marital violence, may want practical information about the divorce laws, and the protection which the court might provide; another may simply want to be listened to; another may wish to understand how such violence came to be a prominent feature in his or her life; and yet another may seek the counsellor's assistance in drawing the marital partner into therapy. The counsellor who 'knows' what the client wants without asking is quite likely to get it wrong.

Sometimes the client's wants and needs may be in conflict. For example, the physically abused client who wishes to draw the marital partner into therapy may be risking immediate damage to life and limb. In such a case, the duty of beneficence or the duty of care requires at least an explanation of the risks involved.

The counsellor is not obliged by the duty of beneficence always to do what the patient, after such discussion, wants. Self-respect for one's own moral autonomy is also important, and there are some actions that one may properly refuse to take because they go against one's own moral principles: one may believe, whether or not the person concerned agrees, that the actions would be too harmful; one may wish to respect the law or one's professional code of ethics; or one may consider them unjust even if they will benefit the patient. None of that, however, negates the prima facie requirement of the obligation of beneficence to find out what the patient wants and to try to meet those requirements.

### Duty to do no harm

A second moral obligation that must temper the duty of beneficence is the duty to do no harm (the duty of non-maleficence). Clinical trials of the efficacy of different therapies for health status, social functioning and quality of life, are therefore essential to inform good practice. It is essential to assess the types, amounts and probabilities of benefit and harm that result or would result from one's therapeutic decisions. As we have indicated, more research is needed into whether counselling actually does benefit patients/clients and, furthermore, into the kinds of counselling that benefit them most, with the least expenditure of resources (see Chapter 4). This is also important in the context of the last of the four principles. Furthermore, there is a major role for clinical audit in establishing whether clients are routinely being benefited with minimal harm, whether referrals are appropriate, whether suicidal risk is assessed, etc.

Further obvious correlates of beneficence tempered by non-maleficence include effective, sympathetic and adequate communication, warmth, concern, politeness and good time keeping. Can we hope that increasing attention is now being paid to these 'quality' issues in the new NHS era of separating purchasing from providing?

*The duty of justice*

Finally, beneficence must be tempered by justice. It seems clear and virtually beyond dispute that if all the available psycho-therapeutic resources were used to provide care for only a favoured section of the sick population (say, the rich), then no matter how beneficent and non-maleficent the care, and no matter how excellent, it would be unjustly, because it was unfairly, provided. Even if we accept that justice must temper beneficence, problems remain about exactly what we mean by justice, as we shall see.

## The principle of non-maleficence

This is sometimes considered as simply an aspect of beneficence (Frankena, 1973). As indicated, beneficence and non-maleficence in clinical practice usually have to be considered and weighed together. However, if we were to try to avoid doing harm altogether, we would have to avoid intervening whenever there was a risk to patients or to others, which would be almost always. Thus the principle of non-maleficence is not absolute; it does not necessarily have priority in cases of conflict with other moral principles; and when there is also a moral obligation of beneficence, the principle of non-maleficence has to be considered in that context.

Counselling carries the risk of potential harm, which would include the risks of exposing anguish and breaking down defences; sometimes, by breaking down fragile defences where little remains to replace them, it risks making people worse off than they were before. Also, there may be competing claims for beneficence and non-maleficence. Benefit to the client may cause problems for the spouse. Similarly, benefit to a parent may cause difficulties for the child. In individual counselling, the primary objective for beneficence is the patient or client. However, in family therapy, the primary objective is the family group.

Furthermore, like the principle of beneficence itself, the principle of non-maleficence may conflict with the principle of respect for autonomy – for example, the patient or client may want to take bigger risks of harm in the pursuit of benefit than the doctor or counsellor would advise. Suppose, for example, a 'borderline psychotic' patient wishes to pursue psycho-therapeutic counselling where the counsellor believes this may provoke a psychotic breakdown. In addition, the principle of non-maleficence may conflict with the principle of justice. (In the Tarasoff case, the client might well have felt and indeed been significantly harmed had the therapist broken confidentiality and compulsorily admitted him into hospital: yet according to two of the three judges, justice to another person (the ex-girlfriend) required that she be protected.)

## The principle of justice

Moving on to the final principle of justice, this may be considered under three headings. The first is fair or just distribution of inadequate resources. The second is fair or just respect for people's rights, and the third is respect for morally acceptable laws (for legal justice). Psychotherapy and counselling are, like all other treatments, competing for resources within the National Health Service. In this competition, it is important to establish the degree of benefit, the number of people, the problems of those people, and the scale of expenditure of resources. It is often assumed that cost does not have anything to do with ethics, but this is a mistaken view because cost makes demands on those who are paying as well as affecting those who do not get resources that have been allocated to others (what economists call opportunity costs); and cost-efficiency means that opportunity cost is reduced, so that more benefit is gained for the same expenditure.

An American philosopher, Robert Nozik (1974), calls taxation legalised theft. The simple fact of a portion of earnings being taken by law in order to benefit others is not, of itself, wrong but it is important to realise that, if there is not a morally acceptable method within a community for obtaining its consent to levy taxes to a certain level, then the autonomy of the taxpayer is being overridden if tax is simply taken, even if that is done to benefit others. In addition, resources having been just obtained, the huge problem remains of how they should be justly distributed. At least part of any satisfactory answer to that question will require evidence that the therapy resourced actually benefits people in need: and the more efficiently it does so (the less wasteful of resources it is) the more justly it can be distributed. This applies as much to counselling and psychotherapy as to any other treatment.

In the context of respect for rights, at first sight there appears to be less of an issue for psychotherapy than, for example, in compulsory admission for treatment, where the individual's right to autonomy is obviously overridden in favour of any rights to health and safety. But rights may insidiously and covertly be overridden. For example, when a therapist decides to use cognitive paradoxical therapy, the patient's right to full knowledge and understanding of the treatment has been overridden. Similarly, only a few patients have access to NHS psychotherapy. Should everyone have an equal right of access?

In the context of respect for morally acceptable laws, it is important to realise that certain aspects of our relationships with our patients are already affected by existing laws within this country. For example, under the Prevention of Terrorism Act we are legally obliged to help the police with their enquiries in the pursuit of terrorists if we are aware that one of our patients is a terrorist. So, if one were doing psychotherapy with a terrorist, one would be obliged under the law to provide information about that client or patient to the police. As a different example, under the Road Traffic Act, we are also required, as is everyone, to provide evidence of identity of any person who has been injured in a Road Traffic Accident.

Now this raises some very deep moral conflicts about personal and professional moral obligations as well as the moral obligations of the community as a whole. How much ought one to obey the law if it conflicts with our obligations to our clients, for example, in relation to confidentiality?

## CONCLUSIONS

It is not possible to set up a precise decision-making process for all ethical decisions which counsellors may have to make, but if counsellors can think through the issues, analysing and assessing the potential relevance of respect for people's autonomy, obligations to benefit and not to harm, and the need for justice, then they will be a long way down the road of taking an ethical decision.

## REFERENCES

Beauchamp, T. H. and Childress, J. F. (1983) *Principles of Biomedical Ethics* (2nd edn), Oxford: Oxford University Press, pp. 265–8.

Frankena, W. K. (1973) *Ethics* (2nd edn), Englewood Cliffs: Prentice-Hall, pp. 45–8.

Hughes, G. (1980) *Moral Decisions*, London: Darton, Longman and Todd, p. 26.

Nozik, R. (1974) *Anarchy, State and Utopia*, Oxford: Blackwell, p. 169.

Paton, H. J. (ed.) (1974) *The Moral Law*, London: Hutchinson University Library, p. 80.

Tarasoff vs. Regents of the University of California, California Supreme Court (17 California Reports, 3rd Series, 425 Decided 1 July 1976). (Quoted in Beauchamp and Childress (1983), pp. 283–4.)

Warnock, M. (1974) *Utilitarianism*, Glasgow: Collins, Fontana, p. 138.

# Chapter 6

# Practical and training issues

*Jill Irving*

Although it is generally acknowledged that counselling has a significant part to play in general practice, many doctors remain uncertain about the benefits and practicability of appointing a counsellor as a member of the primary care team. Opinions range between scepticism and enthusiasm. Some question whether the presence of a professional counsellor undermines the GP's own counselling role, arguing that the research evidence is too limited and inconclusive to convince them otherwise. Others, while acknowledging that counselling like psychotherapy is notoriously difficult to assess, claim that in practice the benefits felt by patients, doctors and other members of the team are sufficient to warrant the acceptance of counsellors as part of the primary care team. However, some of the latter doctors may have held back from employing a counsellor because of practical and training considerations. This chapter examines these issues and how the development of counsellor training and professional standards contribute to this spectrum of opinion.

## TRAINING ISSUES

In the past little information was available to general practitioners on the best ways of using the services of a counsellor, and the range of activities and theories called 'counselling'. Many of the earlier counselling appointments were made through contacts with voluntary organisations or became the consequence of a social encounter. Three doctors who were interviewed about their practice counselling service revealed that one had met his counsellor at a dinner party, another at a cocktail party and the third was married to his! Today, general practitioners have a much firmer base for selecting counsellors since standardised procedures for counsellor training and practice have become established and coordinated information is more readily available. Even so, the professional counsellor is under-represented in general practice. A survey in which 95 of the 97 doctors taking part rated counselling as being important found that only 14 were from practices that employed counsellors and only eight of these used professional counsellors or psycho-therapists. The remaining six used the services of team members who included counselling as part of their job, but whether they were qualified to do so in terms of relevant training and experience was unknown. This raises questions about the training qualifications and experience necessary for counsellors working in general practice.

## Training and recognition of training courses

Counselling is a process which entails a complex coming together of the counsellor's personality, theoretical knowledge, self-awareness, skills and experience. It requires the counsellor to be engaged in a continual process of response decisions whether it be silence or reflection, interpretation or confrontation, where the impetus for the choice of response is based on a theoretical intuitive understanding of human emotions and reactions. The language used needs to be jargon free and the timing of interventions guided by rapport and the ability of the counsellor to empathise with the feelings expressed by the client. Research on counsellor performance and outcome indicates that some counsellors are consistently more effective than others (Truax and Carkuff, 1967). The major ingredient of this effectiveness appears to be the functioning of the counsellor at optimal levels of empathy, warmth and genuineness. While individuals vary in the degree to which they naturally 'possess' these qualities, appropriate training can develop and enhance these skills considerably.

Counsellor trainees are usually selected for training on the basis of the potential suitability of their personality for the work rather than on academic qualifications. During most forms of training, counsellors will receive an overview of the different counselling 'schools' or approaches; be taught counselling theory and developmental processes; take part in experiential work that promotes insight into their own inner life, emotional reactions, prejudices, values, etc.; and work at developing intervention skills in practical work (under supervision) that facilitate changes in the client's attitudes and behaviour. Trainees may choose a course which specialises in a particular form of counselling (e.g. psychodynamic, humanistic, Gestalt, behavioural) and some may go on to seek additional training which extends their knowledge of working with a particular category of client such as family work, the bereaved, or those with alcohol-related problems.

Counsellors can receive their training in a variety of contexts: on a full- or part-time basis; at universities or polytechnics; or with private or charitable organisations such as Relate (previously marriage guidance). These courses, therefore, lead to a variety of qualifications making it very difficult for employers to know whether a counsellor's training, qualifications and experience are sufficient to meet the needs of potential clients.

In order to standardise the situation, BAC introduced a scheme for accreditation of individual counsellors in 1984. BAC also established a scheme in 1988 whereby organisers of courses which train counsellors can apply for Recognition by the Association. Recognition is dependent on the level and quality of the experience and expertise of the staff as well as the course content. Courses that receive recognition will have fulfilled a number of key criteria that provide firm evidence that a high standard of training has been achieved.

## Accreditation of individuals

The British Association for Counselling (BAC) encourages counsellor accreditation to ensure that counsellors meet the recognised standards of training, practice and supervision considered essential for effective counselling. Accreditation is not a professional qualification but is a scheme which provides a standardised presentation of a counsellor's background and commitment to counselling through evidence of practice and training that has met certain criteria. BAC accreditation requires evidence of substantial training which can be gained on one or more courses as long as there is a balance between theory and practice, and the overall training is coherent. It also requires evidence of supervised practice over a period of at least three years as well as commitment to ethical values and ongoing personal and professional development. Individual accreditation runs for five years, after which counsellors may apply for re-accreditation.

It must be remembered that accreditation is not easy to obtain and requires counsellors to have undertaken a number of years of practical counselling experience before they are eligible. Thus, many less experienced counsellors seeking posts will not be sufficiently qualified to obtain accreditation. Other anomalies exist for some counsellors with backgrounds in other professions or a particular training that bars them from BAC accreditation as it now stands. It is therefore possible that some individuals who are not accredited may still have qualifications and experience appropriate for effective working in general practice.

### Experience necessary for general practice

Counsellors in general practice are likely to be referred a wide range of problems, some of which will be related to illness and disability. In some instances, the counselling will be complementary to the GP's or other practice member's involvement, in others it will be an alternative form of therapy. The experience of the counsellor should reflect the needs and interests of the practice and complement the abilities of other members of the practice if counselling is to provide the alternative and complementary form of care needed. The culture and social norms of the patients and the counsellor's awareness and understanding of these also need to be considered.

### PRACTICAL CONSIDERATIONS OF EMPLOYING A COUNSELLOR

### Selection

One source of the names of counsellors (from all backgrounds) is to be found in the *Counselling and Psychotherapy Resources Directory* published annually (see, for example, BAC, 1991). This lists details of organisations and individuals offering a counselling service.

Some GPs advertise for counsellors either in counselling journals or in the national or local press. Examples of job descriptions and conditions of work are given in the *Counselling in General Practice* information folder published by the Royal College of General Practitioners (Staveley, 1992).

### Preparatory work

Reviews of attachment schemes that work well emphasise the need for thorough preparatory work. A clear structure for the counselling work, open to review, needs to be negotiated prior to the counsellor entering general practice. Without this the general practitioners and their team may remain unclear about how and when to make referrals, and counsellors may find the basic requirements for their work – space, quiet and privacy – are lacking. Ideally, counsellors should have a set room but lack of space often means they have to work in doctors' consulting rooms which can increase the difficulty of presenting a role which differs from that of the doctor. Wherever the counsellor works there should be a clear understanding in the practice that he or she is not available and should not be interrupted during the counselling session.

Awareness of how the practice runs, the work of other members of the team, treatment programmes and the effects of psychotropic drugs all need to be part of the counsellor's knowledge. In turn, counsellors have responsibility for 'demystifying' their role by clarifying with the rest of the team the aims and processes of counselling, the skills involved, and their different use of time to avoid the kind of misunderstanding implied by the overheard remark 'they were counselled and they deserved it'.

A formal induction period where the counsellor spends some time with each member of the team is an excellent way for the counsellor and team members to gain understanding of each other's work. The counsellor who spends a session sitting in on a doctor's surgery will directly learn about the stresses and problems faced by GPs. Discussion of patients seen from a counselling perspective will give a clearer idea to the GP of the referral possibilities and what counselling might achieve.

In the initial preparatory meetings, discussions should therefore include:

(a) room arrangements;
(b) the type of counselling carried out, approximate length of

time of the appointments and a rough guide to the number of
sessions carried out with each client;
(c) how to refer patients and what the GP should tell patients (a
leaflet may be desirable);
(d) how appointments will be made – the use of receptionists and
other staff;
(e) issues of confidentiality and record keeping;
(f) the roles of the counsellor in the practice in addition to seeing
patients;
(g) how to get to know each other's ways of working;
(h) the issues of supervision and personal development;
(i) workload and the proportion of counsellor's time spent in
patient contact and in administration, meetings, supervision,
etc.

### Referrals

The referral process is pertinent to outcome and needs both initial
consultation and constant monitoring if it is to succeed. The
process begins as soon as the doctor decides that counselling
might be appropriate for a patient. The way in which the sug-
gestion is made, the information given about counselling and the
counsellor will affect the patient's attitude, hopes and expecta-
tions for outcome. Without sufficient understanding of what is on
offer, patients can feel threatened by the idea of counselling and
may feel rejected by the doctor. Even when the GP has gone to
considerable trouble to gain and give as much information as
possible, the patient may be too anxious 'to hear' or may ask
questions that the GP is unable to answer. Written information
given to the client can be a useful additional resource and has the
advantage of being able to be referred to by the client more than
once. Practice counsellors often write their own leaflets for
clients. This can give a more personal account of counselling and
what it involves, and also serves as an introduction to the person
with whom they will be working.

When making referrals, factors such as time, the relationship
the GP has with the patient and the counsellor and his or her own
counselling skills will all play their part. Agreement will be
needed on several issues, such as: Who is to be told first,
counsellor or client; and does the client make the initial contact
with the counsellor, or vice versa? Should referrals be made by

letter, a simple referral form or verbally? Counsellors have voiced a preference for written referrals because verbal ones are seen to be too ambiguous, complicated by grunts, nods and other non-verbal communications! In practice counsellors find referrals can vary from being the considered choice of the client on the one hand, to the consequence of the doctor exhausting his or her ideas, tests and skills on the other. Most fall somewhere in the middle. Neither referral nor the referral process is likely to work smoothly all the time but key issues of accountability, responsibility and confidentiality can be overlooked if the referral is poorly set up.

The following guidelines have been prepared for doctors who wish to refer patients to a non-medical counsellor.

1. A doctor who delegates treatment or other procedures must be satisfied that the person to whom they are delegated is competent to carry them out.
2. The doctor must retain ultimate responsibility for the management of his or her patients and should be kept informed by the counsellor of any treatment or progress in the patient's condition. The counsellor, too, should be kept informed of any changes the doctor makes in the patient's treatment programme.
3. The doctor should ensure that the counsellor accepts and will abide by the same duty of confidentiality that the doctor observes as well as the counsellor's own professional Code of Ethics and Practice.

## Confidentiality

In practice doctors and counsellors seem well aware of the need to keep communication between them open without affecting the confidential nature of the counselling work. While clients like to know that their confidences will remain 'within four walls' in general, they readily consent to the counsellor discussing their progress with the GP. Most counsellors agree that the boundaries of confidentiality should be outlined with the client at the beginning of counselling to give him or her the opportunity to explore any difficulties this may present – personal material may be very painful and the client's wishes about disclosure need to be respected. In extreme circumstances, such as the client's or another's life being at risk, it may be necessary to break confidentiality – but this is rare. If difficulties do arise they are likely to be due to lack of clarification about the way in which information is shared at the time the attachment is set up. It is an important part of the preparatory work to explore the whole area of confidentiality as GPs retain primary clinical responsibility for the patients they refer to other members of the team. They are also required, by law, to keep accurate records which include the date and reason for referral and any important developments or changes in treatment. Methods of referral, record keeping and how the doctor is kept informed of the patient's progress are all part of ethical practice and need to be considered when the counsellor joins the practice.

## Measuring standards

How counsellors evaluate their work is a question frequently asked by doctors when considering the appointment of a counsellor. While some may argue that counselling is an art rather than a science and cannot be evaluated using scientific methods, many would agree that some system of auditing, correlating subjective ratings with objective criteria, is necessary if counselling is to maintain the credibility it is rapidly gaining and which many doctors, counsellors and clients feel it intuitively deserves.

## Professional development

Those practices with regular meetings will provide counsellors with the opportunity to keep up to date with new developments in the practice, some of which may require a counselling input. Doctors are continually having to respond to challenges in administrative and clinical procedures and, similarly, counsellors need to extend and adapt their skills to the growing needs within the practice and the range of problems that present. Changes in social behaviour and attitudes and the spread of diseases such as AIDS, with all the attendant feelings and concerns, emphasise the need for continued education. Time for active ongoing learning needs to be included in the counsellor's workload. Ethically, counsellors are committed to seeking ways of increasing their professional competence.

Many counsellors consider that ongoing personal therapy (distinct from supervision) is also necessary for their own personal development, and in some counselling courses individuals are expected to have personal therapy during training. Personal therapy, however, is not a requirement of BAC individual accreditation or BAC recognition of training courses.

## Supervision

An effective counsellor has to be able to listen to the client's problem without over-defending or over-identifying or offering salutation (which can be more to do with the counsellor's needs than the client's). It is often stressful work and can rouse deep emotions in those trying to help. Supervision, either with peers or a consultant, enables the counsellor to gain some sort of overview of a case identifying their own personal feelings and professional bias. It provides a continuing process of learning and a form of clinical accountability that counsellors find, ethically and professionally, essential even after years of experience.

Ongoing supervision is a requirement for all BAC members working as counsellors. Guidance as to the appropriate models of supervision are available from BAC. Before a counsellor is employed by a GP, negotiations need to take place on whether the costs of supervision are met by the counsellor and whether the counsellor can include the time for supervision within the number of hours that he or she is employed at the practice.

## Payment

An increasing number of counsellors are being employed by practices with partial reimbursement of their salary through ancillary funding by the Family Health Service Authorities (FHSAs). Staff already in post before the new GP contract will continue to be reimbursed at 70 per cent, but now GPs have to make a case for employing new staff and may not receive 70 per cent of their cost. FHSAs also need proof of suitable training and qualifications before agreeing to the appointment of a counsellor to a practice and the reimbursement of part of their salary. Details of FHSAs known to reimburse practices for employing counsellors can be obtained from the BAC. Alternatively, some GPs fund their counsellors through payments derived from setting up health promotion clinics run by counsellors, although this is now being limited. Counselling in this context can be seen as a method of preventing mental ill health and promoting positive mental health and well being.

Lack of NHS funding for counsellors as legitimate contractual employees has been a major restriction to the employment of counsellors in general practice. Some GPs have employed counsellors on a sessional basis by paying the counsellors themselves. Other counsellors have worked in a general practice on a private basis, charging patients who are referred to them. Self-employed counsellors working on hourly rates are not entitled to sickness benefit, national insurance or a pension and therefore a slightly higher hourly rate of pay may be necessary to offset some of the disadvantages of being self-employed.

The different ways of reimbursing counsellors have made it difficult to establish a national pay scale which includes the standard benefits for NHS salaried staff. Guidelines are now available to help employers negotiate appropriate rates for the type of counselling work undertaken (BAC, 1990). In general, it is considered that salaries for counsellors should be linked to pay scales for other professionals within the field.

*Private counselling*

Some counsellors work in practices where they are paid directly by the client; if so, it is important that patients are made aware that the counsellor charges a fee, or are informed if an alternative service is available under the NHS. This system can work well but this is usually because the counsellor charges relatively low fees or operates a sliding scale. Misunderstandings can occur, such as the GP forgetting to mention the counsellor's fee or the client 'mishearing'. Many of these counsellors are pressing for salaried posts and for payment to be commensurate with their skills and experience although some loss of autonomy and flexibility may occur when they become NHS employees.

If the counsellor is not employed by the practice but is seeing clients on the practice premises, the following points need to be clarified by the doctor with the patient:

1. If the patient has to pay for the counselling service and a similar service is available under the NHS, this must be offered to the patient.
2. The doctor must make it clear to the patient if a fee is to be

charged by the counsellor. The doctor must not receive any financial benefit from this arrangement.

In addition, the doctor should ensure that the counsellor would be held responsible for his or her own acts and omissions and should advise the counsellor to have his or her own insurance cover. BAC encourages all counsellors to have their own insurance cover, and details of insurance companies are available.

## SUMMARY

The increase in counsellor appointments in general practice has given rise to questions about the practicality and appropriateness of including a counsellor in the primary care team. Counselling organisations and associations have responded by producing guidelines and information on the employment of counsellors and the developments in training, standards of practice, support and supervisory structures that have taken place in recent years. Attachment schemes that have worked well have generated a good deal of enthusiastic comment among doctors and counsellors which has informed others interested in appointing a counsellor. Thorough preparatory work and good communication between team members seem to be the cornerstone of success and in practice anxieties about conflict of roles, the referral process and confidentiality are less of a problem than envisaged. Practical disadvantages, such as shortage of rooms, funding and finding time for discussion, cannot be ignored but in general there is a heightened awareness of the beneficial part that counselling can play in general practice. This has stimulated interest in the counselling process and the acquisition of counselling skills by medical personnel.

## REFERENCES

BAC (1990) *Information Sheet 9: Guidelines for the Employment of Counsellors*, Rugby: British Association for Counselling.

BAC (1991) *Counselling and Psychotherapy Resources Directory*, Rugby: British Association for Counselling,

Staveley, R. (1992) 'Appointing a counsellor', in M. Sheldon (ed.), *Royal College of General Practitioners Clinical Series on Counselling in General Practice*, London: RCGP Enterprises.

Truax, C. B. and Carkhuff, R. R. (1967) *Towards Effective Counselling and Psychotherapy Training and Practice*, Chicago: Aldine.

# Chapter 7

# The counsellor as part of the general practice team

*Geoffrey N. Marsh*

One of the things that becomes apparent when a young doctor enters general practice, is his or her lack of expertise and training in coping with the vast volume of sickened and 'dis-eased' people who feel ill but are not in a medical sense clinically ill. Their 'illness' can emanate from a complex mix of psychological, inter-personal, occupational, social, emotional, anthropological, financial and even spiritual factors. In the face of this, some general practitioners retreat into a distancing clinical role, but others accede to being a signpost to those members of their team who can most help the patient. Patently, counsellors are called for. For example, Chester (1971) found that 67 per cent of female petitioners for divorce attended the doctor because they felt their health was affected, and that a further 19 per cent of this large sample could have done, but didn't. Of the people who did attend, 25 per cent consulted their doctor for over two years and a further 16 per cent for between six months and two years.

## ORGANISING A COUNSELLING SERVICE IN A MEDICAL PRACTICE

The writer was particularly fortunate in the setting up of the counselling service in his practice. As he was developing his primary health care team and realising the limitations of his own skills in the counselling area, fortuitously his wife was training to be a marriage counsellor. As a result he became aware of her training and skills and the type of problems she was meeting. At that time (the late 1960s and early 1970s) the marriage counselling offices in many towns were empty, but the surgeries of general practitioners were filled with people seeking that type of help.

Accordingly, meetings were arranged between partners in the practice, the senior members of the local marriage counselling group and one or two of their counsellors. Further meetings took place with the counsellors alone, once both groups could see the potential for having a counsellor in a practice. Thereafter the story was a successful one and many doctors in primary care teams now have counsellors working with them. Accordingly, when the GPs blunder (and that is sometimes an appropriate word) into the psychosocial problems of their patients, they know that skilled people are available and the patient's Pandora's box of problems can be expertly dealt with. As an illustration of its success, in the mid-1970s 25 per cent of the counselling taking place in Cleveland County was for the 15,000 patients in my group practice. Since that time, the need for counselling has become more apparent to the British community, and counsellors in practices, as well as those at centralised counselling premises, are all being stretched.

Initially, the counsellors gave their services free to all patients, supported by occasional donations to the marriage counselling agency. Latterly, many counsellors have 'privatised' their work and charge clients of the practice routinely. More recently, GPs who pay for their counsellor have been eligible for 70 per cent reimbursement of their salaries by the local Family Health Service Authorities. The recent new Contract for General Practitioners may jeopardise this, but the principle of free counselling being available to sickened patients has been established to some extent.

## EVERYBODY A COUNSELLOR

When individual clients ('patients' in the doctor's vernacular) face health care workers of any type, these workers, as well as using their narrow clinical expertise, will frequently find themselves counselling. Health visitors, social workers, CPNs, psychogeriatric nurses, drug and alcohol abuse counsellors and ministers have had special training in counselling. For others who have not, initially they will muddle through as best they can and gradually develop an expertise. This will accrue principally from listening sensitively to the requests, overt or covert, that are being made and to which they are trying to respond. There is an early tendency to be too directive and not allow patients to find their own solutions. There is perhaps a later tendency to be too non-directive, especially to those more deprived members of the community, deprived not only physically and socially, but possibly also mentally. These 'lost', unsure people welcome, and even need, a certain amount of direction from more informed sources.

## THE FUNCTIONING OF THE TEAM

As in many practices, our team meets informally each morning around coffee, and the day's work is shared. It is very much concerned with the day-to-day problems of individual patients. Many teams who have counsellors may not have them working full time. However, they will usually be present at the team meeting on specific days when team members can discuss patients with them. By the same token, social workers, ministers and the more 'part-time' members of the team have regular days when they are known to attend, and relevant problems can be postponed until then. Other more formal meetings can be arranged to discuss the general aims of the team and particularly orientate on counsellors, initially when they join the team, later when their role is being better perceived and finally as the decision is taken to expand their numbers.

The team should function democratically, not hierarchically. It would be invidious of the general practitioner to assume that he or she is the leader of the team when working with independent professional colleagues such as social workers, counsellors, health visitors, ministers of the church. It is better if general practitioners look upon themselves as coordinators, rather than leaders, of the team. It is the problem that the patient presents that leads the team, and those primarily responsible for that problem will for a period lead the team in dealing with it. Hence, leadership can change from week to week as problems come and go.

## THE WORK OF A COUNSELLOR IN A PRIMARY HEALTH CARE TEAM

The work of the counsellor in the practice can perhaps be best described by giving the details of 60 new clients seen by one counsellor in 1988.

## Number of contacts

Of 60 new clients referred in 1988, 35 had concluded their care by mid-1989 and had received 112 sessions – an average of three sessions per client. They included a small number of clients who came once only. Twenty-five clients had not concluded their care by mid-1989. They had 234 sessions, an average of about nine sessions per case, and of course this is still rising. Almost half the clients' partners were also seen.

In accumulating the data for Table 7.1 the counsellor was allowed to choose one major problem, and up to three minor problems, that her 60 clients presented. She perceived that 28 per cent of them had a major problem with their self-image; another third of the clients had this as a minor problem; 17 per cent of the clients had problems with their spouse, or person with whom they were currently living; 15 per cent had problems with separation of various types – divorce, bereavement, or their partner being in prison; and 13 per cent had sexual problems as their major difficulty. Although only 8 per cent had a psychiatric illness as the major problem, a further third had this as a minor problem: hence a considerable number were psychiatrically ill. Seven per cent were receiving counselling in association with a somatic illness – an enormous aid to the doctor – and 8 per cent had physical illness as a minor problem.

A startlingly high 12 per cent of the clients had indicated that they had been sexually abused as children. The recent Cleveland County disclosures seem to be merely the tip of a long-existent iceberg.

*Table 7.1* Problems in 60 counselled patients

| Type of problem | Major | Minor |
| --- | --- | --- |
| Self-image | 17 | 20 |
| 'Spouse' | 10 | 10 |
| 'Separation' | 9 | 5 |
| Sex | 8 | 8 |
| Psychiatric illness | 5 | 20 |
| Physical illness | 4 | 8 |
| Work | 4 | 4 |
| Parents | 2 | 7 |
| Children | 1 | 7 |

## Differences between the 60 counselled patients and controls

Using the practice register, it was possible to match all the counselled patients with someone of the same age and sex who was not receiving counselling. By comparing the counselled patients and their controls it is possible to ascertain any differences between the two groups.

*Table 7.2*  'Somatic' differences between 60 counselled patients and controls (Part 1)

|  | Counselled | Controls |
|---|---|---|
| GP consultations 1988 | 526 | 221 |
| GP consultations 1987 | 333 | 168 |
| Total non-psychiatric admissions | 140 | 77 |
| Average number of outpatient departments attended | 1.5 | 1.0 |

Table 7.2 shows that the counselled group had between two and three times as many GP consultations in the year of counselling (and the year before the counselling) than their controls. Non-psychiatric admissions to hospital were twice as common for counselled patients, and the average number of different types of outpatients departments contacted was 50 per cent higher for the counselled group than the controls. These figures give some indication of the greater utilisation of medical services by the counselled group.

*Table 7.3*  'Somatic' differences between 60 counselled patients and controls (Part 2)

|  | Counselled (%) | Controls (%) |
|---|---|---|
| Smoking | 38 | 32 |
| On long-term drugs | 15 | 12 |
| Attended outpatients department 1988 | 32 | 12 |
| Inpatients 1988 | 7 | 10 |

Table 7.3 shows that the counselled group had more smokers, more people taking long-term drugs for physical illness, and more people attending a non-psychiatric outpatients department

*Table 7.4* Psychiatric differences between 60 counselled patients and controls (Part 1)

|  | Counselled | Controls |
| --- | --- | --- |
| Previous psychiatric illness | 70 | 17 |
| Total psychiatric hospital admissions | 5 | 2 |

than the controls. These figures, along with those shown in Table 7.2, indicate that the counselled patients overall had more physical illness than the controls.

Table 7.4 shows that the 60 counselled patients had had 70 psychiatric diagnoses recorded in their notes over the years compared with only 17 in the controls. The counselled patients were two and half times as likely to have been admitted into hospital for psychiatric illnesses than the controls. In the year of their counselling, 30 per cent of the counselled were on psychotropic drugs and 42 per cent had been on them prior to that year. In the control group, 10 per cent had been on psychotropic drugs in that year and 18 per cent had been on them prior to that year (Table 7.5). None of the controls had attended psychiatric outpatients departments during the year in comparison with 7 per cent of the counselled patients. Thus, in addition to physical illness, the counselled patients were a psychiatrically sicker group than their controls.

*Table 7.5* Psychiatric differences between 60 counselled patients and controls (Part 2)

|  | Counselled (%) | Controls (%) |
| --- | --- | --- |
| On psychotropics in 1988 | 30 | 10 |
| Ever on psychotropics pre-1988 | 42 | 18 |
| Attended psychiatric outpatients department in 1988 | 7 | 0 |
| Attended psychiatric outpatients department pre-1988 | 8 | 5 |
| Psychiatric inpatients in 1988 | 3 | 0 |

## ADVANTAGES OF SURGERY COUNSELLING TO THE DOCTOR AND OTHER TEAM MEMBERS

The great advantage to members of the primary health care team, and perhaps particularly to the patient's doctor, is that the patient receives more expert care from someone specifically trained and experienced in interpersonal relationship problems. It spares the doctor for more purely 'medical' problems. By sharing the burden of these high workload patients with someone else the doctor increases the overall caring yet decreases his or her personal workload. Many doctors have found that, as a result of counselling, patients are able to reduce, stop or decline psychotropic drugs and the problems of drug dependency lessen. By virtue of having a counsellor in their midst and by meeting them at least weekly, team members develop an increased awareness of the interpersonal, marital, sexual and social problems that patients harbour. The counsellor can also help with relationship problems within the team.

## ADVANTAGES OF A COUNSELLOR IN A MEDICAL SETTING TO THE CLIENT/PATIENT

Despite the fact that the clients are not in fact 'sick' in a medical sense, they get to the right agency through the wrong door. Referral to the counsellor can be more immediate, and earlier care of problems can reduce their duration and degree. The surroundings are familiar to them; it is a safe, known environment and also includes an anonymity not present when visiting a formal counselling setting. By and large, the doctors' consulting rooms in which counsellors work are comfortable, pleasant and warm, and ambience can be generated. Ideally, the counsellor should have his or her own room, or at least the same room each week so that rapport can be generated. The patients are encouraged by being referred by someone they trust – their doctor – rather than seeking out help themselves and being unsure of the expertise or suitability of the counsellor concerned.

## CONCLUSION

Overall, the triad of primary health care team member (frequently the general practitioner), counsellor and patient together can cover the whole spectrum of physical, psychological and social dis-ease. Counsellors working in primary health care teams have been one of the major growth areas in recent years. It will be apparent from this chapter why this is so.

## REFERENCE

Chester, R. (1971) 'Health and marriage breakdown: experience of a sample of divorced women', *British Journal of Preventive and Social Medicine* 25: 231–5.

# Chapter 8

# Setting up a counsellor in primary care

## The evolution and experience in one general practice

*Annalee Curran and Roger Higgs*

Names may reveal or conceal, but will always illustrate, just as shadows or highlights create a picture. Primary medical care has collected a string of descriptions which express something of its many-sided character. In Russia there are 'polyclinics', in the United States we find 'family medicine', and in Britain it is 'general practice'. What does each phrase say about its work? We shall return briefly to the American model but British general practice is clear in its statement. It describes work which is essentially pragmatic and responsive – it is there to do things for people – and has a broad, all-embracing approach. It makes an apparently impossible promise: to cater for everything which anyone might decide is appropriately brought to it for attention. It is a world reflected, a microcosm saying (with popular journalism) 'all human life is here' or (if you prefer the more elevated style of the classics) 'nihil humanum a me alienum puto'. It is the first port of call for people who think they are ill, whatever that is, and cannot cope with the illness by their own resources, however small or large these might be.

The ordering of the seemingly limitless quantity of claims thus admitted by this service depends on what is seen to be appropriate, and by definitions of need. As claims on the time increase or change, the service must either turn some away or change itself to become more responsive. This chapter describes one such attempt to respond to a section of need in a new primary care setting in a way which is not now uncommon but which, at the time, was not a regular feature of primary health care in the inner city in south London – the local provision of counselling time and expertise for those whose main concern is a crisis of mind or relationships.

The American phrase 'family medicine' is not often used in Great Britain, in spite of the attractions of the name to describe a section of general practice work. Many feel that it narrows drastically the range of clients and interest of the professionals by excluding in one definition single patients, and those who have yet to set up families. However, even if we reject this description as being too narrow for patient care, it may inadvertently illuminate an important model of professional organisation. The concept of family describes better perhaps than many others the way in which a group or team of people may work together in primary care. This group may need to respond as individuals to the many different problems which patients may bring, and which will require in turn an individual and often very private response; but, in addition, the group also needs the backing, skills, support, and varying perspectives of known and trusted colleagues. The word 'team' is preferred in describing this grouping, as being both more professional and providing a cooler and more objective view. But when it comes to the emotional issues which counselling addresses, both within the consultation and within the professional group itself, the human relationships and reactions bear much more resemblance to family patterns than to any team-playing games known to us. In one sense this concept has never been far from the workplace which we describe, and has provided it with some of its greatest triumphs and some of its most painful failures. In that, it too reflects the peaks and troughs of family life.

The general practice we wish to describe was developed from a single-handed high street inner city practice in the mid-1970s. It served a busy but impoverished area of south central London known for its cohesive working-class culture, which had taken in, in succession to date, peoples from southeast England, then Ireland, then Cyprus and the Caribbean and, more recently, West Africa, Bangladesh and Vietnam. All this, without significantly altering the way in which life was approached, indicates that the culture was strong. This culture included passion, both in terms of commitment to families and to trade, and in terms of violence. It included a healthy cynicism about those who were sent in, or who sent themselves in, from the outside to 'help'. It also included a generosity and an openness about personal problems, about what the real issues were, and about where the needs lay. But in a comparison with a suburban practice, the patients of the practice in this area were found to be three times more likely to have significant non-medical issues (financial, housing, emotional) affecting their health. Where should the expanding practice focus its attention? A Citizens' Advice Bureau lay across the street, a beleaguered borough was struggling to create better housing: but who would offer time for people to reflect on the emotional issues? An early investigator from Medical Films, who recorded a day of consultations in the practice, was amazed. 'It's all about love and death,' he said, as if these were new subjects on the agenda.

The extent to which people need to tell their stories to someone was probably hidden from us initially. This now seems almost a basic human need. We have come to see that the practice of medicine, rather than being 'encumbered' in some way with psychosocial issues (an optional add-on for the professional who has time or interest) is actually a way in which many people have to tell their stories. In some cases it may be the only way in which such people may engage the attention of someone who has time and involvement and enough objectivity not simply to interrupt with their own account. Locally, a story-teller will 'turn round to her and say . . .': it requires a change of position, a revolution indeed, to reveal what is necessary to reveal, to trust enough to turn a potential breakdown into a breakthrough. Groping as we then were towards this concept, at the very beginning we started with bodies. We began with an antenatal group where these issues seemed to be of extreme importance.

Hovering behind concepts like health, relationships and poverty lies the one of class. The NHS had made standard medical care available to all at no cost at point of entry to the system. A generation now intent on throwing this away with extraordinary enthusiasm may not understand the revolutionary importance of this concept. It has huge potential, but is extraordinarily difficult to achieve. Just as the population we served had many more 'life' issues to cope with than their more fortunate suburban counterparts, so we also learned that poverty itself is inextricably linked with disease and illness. But this double jeopardy is linked to a third – that standards under stress in an area of poor resources are pressed downwards. There is no doubt that standards in primary care in inner cities 20 years ago were low, in spite of the work of many individuals to counteract this. The deficiencies of a narrow medical system, made up elsewhere in richer areas by self-help groups, alternative therapies or pressure activities, were left relatively untouched in a locality where survival rather than health was, for many, the prime objective. Not unnaturally, preparation for birth and parenthood was given little space and scant official support. We decided to begin at the beginning.

The success of this work was obvious to us but hard to evaluate objectively. However, it created both a family focus for the practice and a testing bed for some important ideas. All the staff met once a week at lunchtime to discuss our work and we cast the cordon of confidentiality around the whole of this professional group. Trust enabled us to be open about many things (although familiarity helped us to fail to tackle others). But the method was clear. By involving all our staff, including administrative workers who lived locally, the practice was never allowed to stray far from the path of relevance. When one of us wrote an article for the medical press and a counselling agency responded by attaching a trained analytic worker to the practice, the necessity for this approach was underlined. A reflective style did not suit the clients, and few followed up with the therapist. We were faced with a challenge. We knew from all our work that we were not offering what a practice in a more privileged area might do in terms of opportunities for people to make sense of their experiences. But we knew from our medical consultations that there was this need and that people were perceiving it as a need. We knew from the antenatal work that helping people to look at these issues was successful. Our antenatal counselling was developed, slowly but clearly, into a general counselling service based on one-to-one or couple work.

The relevance of this must be underlined, as the approach was consciously eclectic. We knew that to lose some aspects to which clients could relate was to lose their interest. Impassive, uninvolved styles were not understood. More active responses were needed. We had to bend working methods to the needs of the clients, and not vice versa. Later, Cognitive Analytic Therapy (CAT) provided one useful model for the counselling work for patients needing to engage at some depth. But the overall approach has been flexible and intuitive to respond to the particular needs of individual patients.

The attachment has now been set up for several years, and the patterns of work have varied. Some clients refer themselves, some are referred by a member of staff, some involve shared work between a member of staff with the counsellor informally in planning or reporting with the patient's agreement) or formally as a therapy duo. We have achieved a counselling room and a regular system, provided a supervision structure for the counsellors and organised feedback and evaluation of the work with members of the practice. As an illustration, we focus on one year, 1989, as an indication of the extent and variety of the work carried out.

## NUMBER OF COUNSELLOR CONTACTS

In 1989, 98 people (81 women and 17 men) made appointments to be seen by the counsellor. Fourteen did not take up their first appointment at all, and the remaining 84 were seen for an average of 3.5 sessions each. This figure includes six people who were ending or coming for a follow-up from the previous year, and 16 who were seen for a maximum of two sessions and then referred on to other agencies (CPN, psychiatric outpatients, short-term therapy at the local hospital, private therapy, or community counselling service), 34 people for whom between one and four sessions were enough to give them an opportunity to air their problems and find some alleviation of their distress, and 28 people who were seen for more than four sessions.

## PATHWAYS TO COUNSELLING

There was a broad range of problems which led people to seek counselling, although common themes emerged. As elsewhere in primary care, the problem for which a patient is referred to counselling is often only the tip of an iceberg which is far deeper and more complex than the presenting problem. In societies where psychotherapy is in vogue, no reasons are required for a client to start this work. But most people in south London, especially if they come via the GP, seem to feel that they need a legitimate 'problem', or passport, in order to get counselling help. In general practice, some patients present to the GP problems which are purely physical, while others already guess that their bodies are speaking for their psyche in some way. In either case, the presenting problem acts as a way of asking for help and it is usually necessary, without denying the meaning of the symptom or the fear it often engenders, to move to the underlying causes as quickly as possible. Also, sometimes a patient is referred for a particular problem, but when more time is spent it emerges that there are other significant problems which had not originally been voiced. An example:

A young woman was referred for depression and sleeplessness, but was also severely bulimic, although she had not initially been able to say so. Another woman, referred because of anxiety and panic attacks, revealed later that she was involved in obsessive washing and cleaning rituals.

## PROBLEMS IN CONTEXT

When we examine overall the people seen in that year, it seems as though the most common difficulties in order of prevalence were: distressing questions about 'who am I?' or 'where am I going?', depression, relationship difficulties, anxiety and stress, panic attacks, unresolved childhood experiences, bereavement, low self-esteem, eating disorders, social isolation, uncontrollable anger, paranoid feelings, issues around pregnancy and abortion, and alcohol abuse. There were a number of people who had sexual difficulties or anxiety about their sexual identity. About eight people in the year seemed to be borderline or possibly psychotic and required referral to the CPN or psychiatric outpatients. Other problems which emerged in some people were previous suicide attempts or self-harm, previous rape, coping with chronic physical illness, and coping with a terminally ill or dementing relative.

## OUTCOME

By the end of 1989, 27 people had successfully completed whatever plan we had agreed on. For some, this may have been a single session which sufficed to clarify things for the client, but for the majority the agreed plan would have involved four to 16 sessions. Eighteen people were still engaged in counselling as the year came to an end and work continued with them into the following year. Fourteen people had been referred on, some after one session of assessment, but some after a few sessions of exploring possibilities and helping the patient to decide what was required regarding counselling or psychotherapy. There were two people to whom counselling was suggested, in general terms, and seven who could recognise that they needed to do therapeutic work, but for whom the time did not seem right. This was often because of resistance. Three people made a unilateral decision to stop and another three stopped because 'everything was fine now'. For four people, life events such as moving or the birth of a baby stopped the counselling. With six people, the agreed plan faded out, with repeated communications and non-attendance and, finally, lack of response.

## THE DILEMMA OF COMMUNITY CARE

On a broader scale, however, many of those who fail to complete a course of counselling subsequently re-present, perhaps because they are more ready to continue with therapeutic work at a later stage, or because further experiences have brought them to realise the need to 'grasp the nettle'. Working in general practice makes it a lot easier to pick up the threads and continue work with a patient. Although explicitly finite plans are made for a counselling series with patients at the outset, they do have an understanding that the counsellor is part of the primary care team at the surgery where they are most likely to come if crises occur in their life. It is important to be aware of maintaining the balance between being too readily available to people and being too inflexible about the limit of time to be offered to them. It is clearly not helpful to the counselling process to be an ever-present, universal agony aunt to whom people can drop in for a 'pick-me-up' whenever things get a little difficult. People engaged in counselling should have a sense of commitment to the sessions and their purpose, and be aware of the boundaries. On the other hand, the reality of life is such that many people may need to make several 'circuits' of the same basic difficulty before they are really ready to face the underlying pain in their lives and to begin to find ways of changing.

## TIME LIMITATION

Time is inevitably a problem when one is working in an NHS setting where the demand seems to be limitless. One is acutely aware of this demand working in a general practice where people have easy access to their general practitioner and other members of the team, and where their difficulties are likely to be picked up at an early stage. We have, therefore, had to make the decision that the counsellor can normally only offer people time-limited, short-term counselling. There are very rare situations where on-going work is clearly imperative. However, offering time-limited counselling or therapy to a patient means that it is vitally important to get to the core of their pain and work at a deep level, rather than just offering a tiny and, perhaps, superficial bite of something which is actually meant to be much longer. In this regard, using the particular model of short-term therapy developed as Cognitive Analytic Therapy has proved useful and fruitful.

## COGNITIVE ANALYTIC THERAPY

This model of work, originated by Dr Anthony Ryle, was used with 19 of the patients seen in 1989. It aims to help the patient and therapist focus on the underlying repeated patterns of belief, thought and action in which the patient has become stuck, and which repeatedly cause distress and prevent the patient from living a fulfilling life. For example, people who continually need to please others and to be 'doormats', out of a sense of low self-worth, will invariably be taken advantage of and put upon by others. This, in turn, will make them feel angry and resentful that their own needs never receive attention. The anger might burst out irrationally, thus reinforcing the idea that they are bad and worthless and pushing them into the vicious circle again of bending over backwards to please others. When patients can see how they are caught in a pattern such as this, and why that has come about (usually because of experiences in earlier life), and when they begin to monitor how it applies in their life, they can begin to challenge the underlying assumption of unworthiness and define ways of breaking the inevitability of the vicious cycle.

Another example of these underlying patterns is where people feel they are caught between two poles of a dilemma, such as 'either I keep my feelings bottled up or I let my feelings out and risk being rejected, making a mess or hurting other people'. With one patient who was suffering from bad headaches, we found that rephrasing this dilemma as 'either a tortoise hiding in my shell and missing out on life, or a raging, angry tiger who could hurt and destroy others' was helpful. He was firmly stuck in the tortoise side of the dilemma because the only alternative he saw was the raging tiger and his headaches represented all the anger he was keeping firmly under wraps. With the counsellor he explored the possibility of his being a strong but gentle horse, who could stand up for himself without hurting others.

## Reformulation

Having elicited the underlying patterns which seem to be operating in a patient's life through looking at his or her presenting problems, hearing the patient's story, setting self-monitoring homework tasks and beginning to interpret the therapeutic relationship, a reformulation of the problem is then shared with the patient in the form of a written piece of prose. This aims to name his or her core pain, to get an understanding of where that has come from and particularly to show how the individual has become stuck in these repeated, faulty patterns as an attempt to avoid and survive the inner pain, whether that be fear of abandonment, unexpressed anger, longing for love, guilt, or overwhelming sadness. This reformulation, which uses the patient's own words and images as much as possible, then acts as a scaffolding in which the patient can more safely begin to experience the deep, hidden feelings while, at the same time, begin to make changes in his or her life on a more cognitive level. The patient of the tortoise and the tiger, for example, was able to get in touch with the rage he had felt at the birth of his sister when he was 4 years old; this was never allowed expression because his was such a 'happy, calm family'. After reformulation, he was also able to stand up for himself a bit more at work, discovering that, if he asked colleagues not to dump their equipment on his work bench, they would respect his wish without becoming unfriendly.

## Ending therapy

The focus during the therapy is maintained by rating the main areas of faulty thinking in each session and by enlisting the active involvement of the patient in homework tasks. At the end of the therapy 'goodbye letters' are exchanged between patient and therapist which serve as a summary of what has been achieved from the point of view of both patient and therapist. It also reinforces the 'tools' which patients have hopefully gained and which can then continue to be used as they become, to some extent, their own therapists. Excerpts from some patients' goodbye letters illustrate this.

> I am writing to say thanks because you have told me about things that I'll always have. . . . It's great to think I can do things, that there is potential instead of feeling completely stuck and weighed down with no way out, that I have the ability to make things change rather than just being manoeuvred by what's happening around me.

> When I first came to see you I was suffering from panic attacks and anxiety. I felt worthless and that I wasn't taken seriously especially where my symptoms were concerned. I really felt that I was going mad. . . . As the weeks went by and each session brought out my feelings about my childhood and my family, I began to become calmer, more confident and the panic attacks lessened, becoming more infrequent. . . . For the first time in years I feel I have something to look forward to, a future with aims and goals which before would have seemed impossible. . . . There are times when I feel the old anxieties coming back, but I don't panic any more. I deal with them now so they don't hurt me.

> . . . and it helped me to unburden myself by talking to you and to now not feel so guilty about all what has happened years ago. I still have a bad day now and again but I seem more able to cope with it. I thank you again for listening to me.

> . . . and in the future it will be a lot easier to make sure I don't fall into any more traps as I have done in the past. Your mini-biography was very accurate and quite painful to hear at first, but it helped me accept the fact that there has been sadness, but before I refused to accept it.

### Naming the pain

It has been very fulfilling to work with patients using CAT, particularly because it enables the 'core pain' to be named meaningfully and early in the therapy, and because it empowers the patients to continue the work on their own. It also has a practical value in the cases where a patient does, perhaps, come back months or years later because both patient and counsellor have the 'reformulation' available and ratings and goodbye letters as a concrete reminder of the shared understanding.

## OTHER MODELS

With the majority of patients, CAT is not used at present. This may be due to time pressure, and patients for whom CAT would be beneficial can be referred to the local hospital where CAT is also offered. But there are cases in which other approaches seem to be more appropriate. The greatest advantage of having a free rein in decision making about what to offer patients is that intuition can be followed and a patient can be offered what seems specifically relevant. Sometimes supportive counselling seems to be what people need. This may be during a difficult patch in their life, or to cope with long-standing difficulties which cannot be changed. A series of four to six sessions would usually be offered, or people might be seen once a month over a longer period.

Bereavement counselling needs to be offered quite specifically. It could be that a patient has recently lost someone close and needs a space to be able to express all the range of feelings he or she may be having. Sometimes, the death may have been some time before, but, for whatever reason, the patient was unable to grieve properly at the time. And then there may be situations of grieving for a miscarried baby or the more complex difficulty of unexpected mourning after an abortion. There can also be bereavement for a lost breast after mastectomy or for a loss of lifestyle, for whatever reason. It is necessary to be inventive with people who are stuck in their grief, particularly if they seem unable to say goodbye to and let go of the person who has died, while still keeping the good memories of the reality of the relationship with that person. Sometimes it is necessary to devise a ritual of some kind, perhaps a visit to the grave, or private ceremony in a special place, or create a collage of photographs.

There are situations where the style of counselling which has been found helpful can seem almost flippant. An example:

A woman of 60 was seen for several sessions. She seemed unable to get over the loss of her husband and her mother who died within a fairly short space of time. She had no children and felt that her siblings weren't close to her. But she had clearly had an almost 'fused' relationship with both her mother and husband. She developed physical symptoms such as aching legs and breathlessness, but no matter how much the counsellor tried to get beyond these symptoms, and the immediate grief, she seemed unable to use any kind of insight into her overall situation in life. Very little progress was made during the first series of four sessions. About a year later she was referred again by a different doctor, having in the meantime developed diabetes. All the old physical symptoms were still there, plus some new ones, and the same tearfulness about her husband and mother. It seemed that nothing had changed. Perhaps the counsellor could have persisted in an attempt to make her face up to her lifelong need for dependency and to the fact that she had never really been a person in her own right. But it seemed doubtful that this would be achieved, and there was the added problem of her painful legs and the difficulty in getting to the surgery. So the counsellor tried to explore whether there were any small ways in which her present life could be altered to make it more bearable.

She said how much she enjoyed playing Bingo, how good she was at 'playing a number of books at once' and about the friends she made there. She hadn't been since her husband died. The journey to her favourite Bingo Hall was feasible by bus and so the counsellor arranged to telephone her in a fortnight. At that point, she had in fact been to Bingo and had 'thoroughly enjoyed' herself. She is now contacted by phone every six weeks and it seems that she has made great progress in overcoming her social isolation and is far less engrossed in her feelings of self-pity.

## WORK WITH THE TEAM

We have presented a glimpse of a year's counselling work with the patients of one general practice. However, there are other roles which the counsellor may be asked to assume within the primary care team. There is an emotional content to any interaction between professional and patient. Even the person presenting with a sprained ankle is also 'presenting' how it feels, how he or she copes with the pain, how it affects his or her life, how it perhaps touches on other experiences of accident, and so on. None of these may be voiced overtly during a consultation, but an intuitive GP will know that this potential agenda is there. Obviously when a patient visits the GP because of more serious illness, or because of emotional upset, that large agenda is all the more likely to come into play. No matter how directly this is actually addressed by the patient and the GP, the patient's experience is inevitably going to touch that of the doctor. GPs deal with this in different ways across the spectrum, from fervent denial of being touched personally in any way, to over-involvement and identification which may lead to collusion or over-dependence. It may sometimes be useful for a GP or other worker to be able to talk about patients with the counsellor to help to clarify these issues. So it may happen quite frequently that the counsellor will be 'involved' with a patient who is not actually met, where the work is more that of a supervisor, giving the GP, health visitor, nurse or receptionist an opportunity to think aloud, and perhaps be able to reflect back to them what might be going on in their interaction with a patient, and exploring different ways of approaching this.

There are also, inevitably, occasions for the counsellor working in the surgery with a group of people whom he or she knows well when one of the other members of the team may need to unload some personal distress or difficulty, and will turn to the counsellor. This happens spontaneously: it has not been set up as a formal part of the counselling role, but it does seem to be a valuable aspect of working in a group. The counsellor would not engage in any counselling work as such with colleagues, but it feels appropriate to provide a safe space for them in which they can do some initial unburdening and explore possible avenues for further help. People may gravitate to the counsellor because of his or her role with patients. Once professionals realise their need to discuss the effects of their work at this level, there may be reciprocal interactions between members of a healthy professional 'family'. In an environment of trust between colleagues, individuals could ideally turn to others in the team when they are in need of support or comfort.

After working in this general practice for some time a counsellor wrote some personal thoughts:

In my experience of working in a general practice, I have found that it is vital to be accessible to the patients whom I see. By this I do not mean being readily available to them at every turn (which can in fact be counter-productive in counselling work), but rather being able to hear people on their terms and in their language so that they can be aware of the sort of empathetic listening which should be the basis of a fruitful therapeutic relationship. I believe very strongly that the experience of emotional joy or distress knows no distinctions up and down the socio-economic ladder, and that what people long for (no matter where they come from) is the words to give name and meaning to their experience. The counselling process, for me, involves helping people to find their own words (words of the heart, rather than the head, which may even be visual images). In doing so there is a way in which the apparently mundane and limited experience of a particular patient, even with its immediate unhappiness, can be expanded to embrace the most profound insights and depths of human feeling.

## END PIECE

Each practice or primary care team is an organic unit with professional skills and resources of a pattern particular to itself, facing the needs of a unique population. However important the development of objective standards in counselling work in primary care, the style and methods of response of the team, and the counsellor in particular, must fit the needs of the locality and be congruent with the culture of the practice. A commitment to counselling implies not only a commitment to growth within the consultation, but also a commitment to reflection, growth and development within the team itself.

# Chapter 9

# Evaluating counsellor placements

*Roslyn Corney*

When counsellors are attached or employed, it is important to take the opportunity to examine the value and effectiveness of the placement. As resources are becoming increasingly limited, adding any additional members to the primary care team needs to be assessed and evaluated carefully. However, evaluation may be particularly worth while in the field of counselling as it can aid future decisions regarding the best way to use the counsellor's limited time in the surgery. For example, an evaluation may find out that the consultative role of the counsellor (giving other team members support or advice regarding their patients) is as valuable as the counsellor seeing clients directly. Alternatively, an evaluation can suggest that running a group for clients (for example, a support group for those wishing to withdraw from tranquillisers) is more cost-effective than seeing patients individually. Assessments may also yield information on the types of patients who seem to benefit most from seeing a counsellor as well as those who find it difficult to accept this type of help.

## WHAT IS THE PURPOSE OF THE ATTACHMENT?

Before any evaluation is attempted it is very important to consider carefully the aims of having a counsellor attached to the practice. What does the practice hope to achieve by having a counsellor attached and how can they measure whether these aims have been achieved? It is possible that different members of the practice may have different aims for the counsellor. Initial clarification may be of use in reducing any misunderstandings that might occur. Essentially, those attempting any evaluation should ask themselves the following questions: Exactly what am

I seeking to measure? Precisely what information do I need? How can I best obtain that information?

## CLIENTS REFERRED AND THE WORKLOAD OF THE COUNSELLOR

Standard records should be kept on all clients referred irrespective of whether or not they turn up for counselling (examples of forms that may be used are given in the appendix). Demographic details are important, the client's age, marital status, occupation, number of children living at home, psychological, social and health problems and reason for referral. If referral agents complete a standardized form on referral, these data can be used. Additional information may also be collected depending on the aims of the counsellor, the attachment and the area the practice covers.

The counsellor can also keep records on the number of times each client was seen, any appointments not kept and length of contact made. These records can be used to give some assessment of the workload and working patterns of the counsellor (see appendix).

Information on non-attenders is also important. If many clients fail to turn up, the referral process may need to be examined. Alternatively, the types of patients being referred may not be appropriate for counselling. Details of clients who only attend once and fail to attend for follow-up appointments may also shed light on the counselling and referral process.

## SUBJECTIVE ASSESSMENTS FROM THE COUNSELLORS AND OTHERS

After the client has been seen by the counsellor, a number of other details and opinions can be collected. This could include the client's and the counsellor's perceptions of the problems presented, the plan of action, whether this was agreed with the client as well as the client's motivation to be helped.

After cessation of counselling, details can be collected on the counsellor's perception of whether the client was helped, brief details of the therapy, any arrangements made for future involvement, and the counsellor's final perception of client's motivation to be helped. Records can be supplemented by other involved team members (for example, the referral agent) filling in a short form of their opinion of any improvement or changes they have perceived in the client.

If these details are routinely collected, an overall picture of the success of the attachment can be obtained. Details such as which patients turn up for counselling and which patients were perceived as having been helped will become the basis of making a more objective assessment of the value of the attachment rather than relying on subjective opinions and attitudes. A number of studies of referrals have been reported in the literature which give guidelines on the type of information to collect (Marsh and Barr, 1975; Cohen, 1977; Meacher, 1977; Anderson and Hasler, 1979; Waydenfeld and Waydenfeld, 1980; Martin and Mitchell, 1983; Martin and Martin, 1985).

## CHANGES IN ATTITUDES TOWARDS COUNSELLING

In order to obtain any measures of changes in the attitudes of members of the team towards counselling and counsellors it is important to carry out the initial assessment prior to the start of the attachment. A second assessment can be obtained at a reasonable period after the beginning of the placement. These assessments can be collected by questionnaire, interview or by group discussion (Meacher, 1977; Ashurst and Ward, 1983). Some investigators have also asked random samples of patients their views of the value of having a counsellor in the practice. The results overwhelmingly suggest that patients regard it as beneficial and are generally in favour of self-referral as well as referral from members of the primary care team.

## CLIENT'S VIEWS

Clients seen by the counsellor can be asked to give their views of whether the counselling helped. Clients who do not turn up for further counselling can also be contacted, although it is likely that the response rate for this group of patients is likely to be low. However, to obtain unbiased answers, the questionnaires or interviews should be conducted by an individual independent from the counsellor or the practice. If an individual working from the practice is involved, it is often better to use anonymous questionnaires sent to clients through the post (an example of a questionnaire that could be used is given in the appendix). Any demographic data which are considered to be important in analysing the results can be obtained by asking a few additional questions on the questionnaires and the reasons for doing this explained to the respondent.

Semi-structured interviews are better for obtaining qualitative information including feelings, beliefs and values but these are more time consuming than the use of questionnaires. A combination of qualitative and quantitative data can be obtained if questionnaires are sent to all clients and a smaller sample (randomly chosen) are interviewed.

While client questionnaires are valuable, their bias has to be considered. For example, many clients may not wish to say anything against someone associated with their doctor, especially when they appreciate the time and effort spent on them. Other clients may never be satisfied with any help received from professionals. Clients' views are also not definitive evidence of outcome as clients do not know what would have happened if they had not seen a counsellor. Nevertheless, clients' views can be important and valid sources of feedback and yield tentative information on the clients who benefited most from counselling. They may also be helpful in clarifying those therapeutic methods that are more acceptable to clients, and the types of treatments that are of most benefit.

Client feedback may also include other questions to evaluate the service, satisfaction with access, hours, waiting lists, reception procedures, concerns over confidentiality, etc.

## MEDICAL UTILISATION RATES AND COST-EFFECTIVENESS

One argument in favour of placing a counsellor in the practice is that it may reduce the number of times the client visits the doctor or uses other health care services. This offsets some of the costs of the counsellor. For each client referred to the counsellor, a set time period before counselling is compared with a similar time period during and after cessation of counselling. Thus details of numbers of attendances, prescriptions written and referrals made to other agencies are collected from the medical notes or by placing special cards in the notes on referral.

Many studies have indeed found a reduction in visits to the

doctor after cessation of counselling, in comparison with the period before referral as well as a reduction in the prescribing of psychotropic drugs and a reduction in referrals to psychiatrists (Marsh and Barr, 1975; Cohen, 1977; Meacher, 1977; Waydenfeld and Waydenfeld, 1980; Illman, 1983; Corney, 1986).

Proving that counselling is cost-effective is likely to be extremely difficult. Reductions in psychotropic drug prescriptions and attendance figures have been used to argue the case of the cost-effectiveness of counselling but it is difficult to argue this without the use of a control group of patients who were not referred to a counsellor. Analyses of costs are extremely difficult to carry out. They should take into account and try to cost the greater sense of well-being of the individuals concerned after counselling and the effects on their families and their physical health. However, normally, benefits are often only measured in terms of tangible outcomes such as reduced prescriptions and fewer attendances.

The use of these limited indices is unlikely to show that a counsellor is cost-effective. For example, if an attachment is to be successful, the reduction in GP time spent may only be minimal as doctors need to spend time discussing patients with the counsellor and possibly becoming involved in joint sessions. A counsellor in a practice may also encourage and stimulate others to do some 'counselling' themselves either after the surgery or by arranging a few longer appointment sessions. This will not normally decrease the doctor's workload. Because of these difficulties, practices should collect additional information regarding attitude change and clients' views in order to justify the value of the attachment rather than only measuring costs.

Reductions in medical utilisation and in psychotropic drug prescriptions have also been used to indicate that counselling has been of value in improving the client's health. However, caution does need to be exercised. Doctors may use counselling as an alternative to a psychotropic drug prescription and this, rather than the client getting better, may explain the reduction in drug prescription. In addition, a reduction in GP attendances may not always be positive. In some clients, ongoing medical contact for physical ailments may be important and in some cases a counsellor who is concerned about a client's health may suggest that the client contact his or her doctor. It is also likely that there will be fewer visits in the period after a referral than the period before it. Patients are normally referred at a crisis point in their lives when attendances are more likely to be frequent.

## CASE CONTROL STUDIES

Counsellors and therapists can benefit and learn by carrying out their own research on their clients. This can be done by performing simple case control studies, obtaining baseline ratings before treatment and then comparing them with follow-up scores. In behaviour therapy, these ratings are often routinely collected. While this is a fairly simple task with some disorders, for example, phobias, it is much more difficult with more complex problems including family and interpersonal situations.

Some investigators have compared the progress of the counselled clients with a matched group of patients selected from the medical register (as in Chapter 7). These can be useful for direct comparisons between the clients referred and the 'normal' population. However, the controls are usually only matched in terms of age and sex and not in terms of their psychosocial problems. This makes it difficult to compare outcome over time between the counselled groups and the controls.

## THE CLINICAL TRIAL

In clinical trials, the outcome of one group of patients receiving treatment is compared with the outcome of another group who receive either no treatment or treatment of another kind. Ideally, patients entering into clinical trials should be randomly allocated to the experimental group or the control group so that there are no initial differences between the two groups.

The need for a control group is crucial as high proportions of patients with depression and anxiety (those patients most likely to be referred to a counsellor) will get better and resolve their problems themselves without outside help. Patients will normally be referred to a counsellor at a point when their problems are most likely to be at their worst. This means that many patients are likely to show some improvement at a follow-up interview, even without treatment. To show that counselling is effective, we have to obtain better rates of improvement in those receiving counselling than in those receiving routine GP treatment.

Clinical trials can take up considerable resources and are often difficult to undertake. It is advisable for practitioners who wish to undertake a trial to contact researchers with experience in this area.

Problems that arise in setting up a trial include the following: specifying the criteria of improvement which should be used, deciding on when the assessments should be undertaken, and which assessments should be used. There are also problems of deciding the treatment (if any) the control patients should receive and whether any ethical issues are involved if treatment is denied.

Deciding on what constitutes improvement may involve a number of value judgements. For example, in marital therapy does effectiveness mean an improvement in the clients' physical and mental health or is it more important to keep clients' marriages together? Marriage guidance counselling may not reduce the number of marriage breakups, for example. An effective marriage guidance counsellor may ease the process of a couple splitting up so that a woman trapped in a destructive marriage is given the support to start a new life for herself.

Measures of outcome should include objective ratings if at all possible; this can include health records and measures of illness behaviour. The majority of studies also include details made during an assessment (given usually pre- and post-treatment). This can include social ratings, scores on psychiatric or psychological ratings and estimates of physical and psychosomatic symptoms. Details of alcohol and drug intake can also be collected.

Subjective information can also be important – the client's own views of help received, his or her relatives' views. It is also important to collect an assessment from the GP and others (i.e. the health visitor) on any perceived improvement in the client. Although most clients will indicate that they were satisfied with the help received, subjective accounts sometimes yield insights into what clients find most or least helpful.

## SUMMARY

In planning an evaluation of counselling in general practice, the following areas should be considered by GPs and counsellors:

(a) an assessment of the counsellor's roles;
(b) the characteristics of patients referred to the counsellor;
(c) the characteristics of patients who fail to attend or drop out of treatment;
(d) the type of 'treatment' offered to clients and the number of sessions given;
(e) the counsellor's views on the effectiveness of the treatment with specific clients;
(f) the views of other professionals on the effectiveness of the counsellor with specific clients;
(g) the views of clients referred to the counsellor on effectiveness
(h) whether the provision of counselling alters the workload of other professionals;
(i) an assessment of attitudes of other professionals and clients towards counselling in general.

## REFERENCES

Anderson, S. and Hasler, J. (1979) 'Counselling in general practice', *Journal of the Royal College of General Practitioners* 29: 352–6.

Ashurst, P. M. and Ward, D. F. (1983) *An Evaluation of Counselling in General Practice*, Final report of the Leverhulme Counselling Project. Report available from the Mental Health Foundation, London.

Cohen, J.S.H. (1977) 'Marital counselling in general practice', *Proceedings of the Royal College of Medicine* 70: 495–6.

Corney, R. (1986) 'Marriage guidance counselling in general practice', *Journal of the Royal College of General Practitioners* 36: 424–6.

Illman, J. (1983) 'Is psychiatric referral good value for money?', *BMA New Review* 9: 41–2.

Marsh, G. N. and Barr, J. (1975) 'Marriage guidance counselling in a group practice', *Journal of the Royal College of General Practitioners* 25: 73–5.

Martin, E. and Martin, P. M. L. (1985) 'Changes in psychological diagnosis and prescription in a practice employing a counsellor', *Family Practice* 2: 241–3.

Martin, E. and Mitchell, H. (1983) 'A counsellor in general practice: a one-year survey', *Journal of the Royal College of General Practitioners* 33: 366–7.

Meacher, M. (1977) *A Pilot Counselling Scheme with General Practitioner: Summary Report*, London: Mental Health Foundation (unpublished).

Waydenfeld, D. and Waydenfeld, S. W. (1980) 'Counselling in general practice', *Journal of the Royal College of General Practitioners* 30: 671–7.

# Chapter 10

# The future of counselling in primary care

## Vivienne Ball and Roslyn Corney

At the present moment, the future of counsellors in primary care seems more certain than ever before. General practitioners are pressurising the FHSAs to fund services to the practice. Now that the majority of practices have one or more practice nurses in post, surveys of GPs' views indicate that GPs next prioritise the need for help with managing the psychosocial component of their workload (Corney and Thomas, 1992).

A number of issues will be considered in this chapter: funding the service, the FHSAs' involvement, evaluation, setting standards, and the training needs of counsellors.

### FUNDING THE SERVICE AND THE ROLE OF THE FHSA

FHSAs and DHAs (District Health Authorities) are responsible for the planning and evaluation of services in their area and for making sure that the needs of the population are met. Determining the level of need in this area is not easy, depending on the demography of the area and the services currently available. The role of the secondary sector also needs to be appraised in order to plan for the care of people with emotional difficulties. Thus FHSAs and DHAs will need to consider whether community mental health teams are focusing on the more severely ill and the psychotic disorders rather than on this patient group, whether community mental health centres are well developed in the area and have 'walk in' clinics, and whether social services or psychologists are catering for this group in the population.

FHSAs must consider certain issues, such as whether they should ringfence money specifically for counselling in general practice. If they agree on this, it is still difficult to ascertain how much 'counselling time' a practice needs to meet the health requirements of a community and what priority should be given to counselling services in general practice. One recent document suggests that 20 hours per week is suitable for 9,000 patients (Curtis-Jenkins, 1991); however, another report suggests that one hour per week per 1,000 patients would be adequate (Jewell, 1992). In addition, FHSAs need to ensure that they have the personnel available to coordinate these developments as an understanding of the role of counselling is vital if the scheme is to be a success. Supporting practices and counsellors in what will be a new venture for many is crucial.

It is important to ensure that counsellors employed in general practice are well equipped to carry out their tasks in a professional manner. A stable source of funding will mean that general practices can attract well-qualified and experienced counsellors. Many counsellors are currently employed in general practice under the scheme for health promotion clinic payments. This is not a satisfactory way of long-term funding of professionals who wish to have some form of security and it will not encourage counsellors to undergo lengthy and costly specific training for general practice work. In addition, the health promotion scheme is currently under review and it seems likely that changes may be made in the amount of revenue available as well as the type of payments made.

A more satisfactory arrangement is for counsellors to be reimbursed under the ancillary staff scheme, thus demonstrating more of a commitment to counselling. At the present time, FHSAs vary according to whether they fund counsellors under the ancillary scheme and what they fund. Some fund only the counsellor's time spent in direct contact with patients while others fund time spent on both practice administration and on discussing patients with other members of the primary care team. While ongoing supervision is essential for all counsellors, only some GPs and FHSAs fund the cost of this plus the time involved.

GPs willing to employ a counsellor need to find out about the local policy on the employment of counsellors. If the FHSA has no policy, the GP may need to prepare a case for developing a counselling service and give specific details of the arrangement planned. A useful guide on how to do this is available from the Counselling in Primary Care Trust (address: see Curtis-Jenkins, 1991).

## TRAINING AND AGREEING ON A NATIONAL STANDARD

What standards are necessary in primary care? At the present time, BAC accreditation is the only current professional standard that we have and many FHSAs regard that counsellors must be eligible for this accreditation to be employed. These counsellors are highly experienced. To be eligible they have to fulfil one of three conditions: (a) to have completed a BAC recognised training course and have undertaken 450 hours' supervised counselling practice over three years; or (b) to have undertaken 450 hours' training (250 theory and 200 skills development) in addition to the 450 hours' counselling practice; or (c) to have had 10 years' experience of counselling ( at a minimum of 150 hours per year) including ongoing supervision. While these standards are high, EC standards (for psychotherapy) are even higher although negotiations are taking place for a standard for counselling.

A standard should reflect the competency required in order to fulfil a role or function. The role of the counsellor in primary care is potentially very diverse, so FHSAs, GPs and counsellors need to clarify the responsibilities and duties. However, we need to determine the core function and agree on a national standard. A working group involving BAC, the Royal College of GPs, Relate, the British Psychological Society and other organisations are exploring this currently. There is a great need for a national forum in order to give information to FHSAs and GPs and to set specific guidelines and certain minimal standards. At the present time, there is little to guide FHSAs in this area.

At present, there are few training courses specifically geared for counsellors working in primary care. Some areas of the country have a wide choice of training courses for individuals; however, other regions have very little to offer in terms of quality. Training needs to include theory, skills, practice and supervision, in order to provide the balance required for this role. Post-basic training specifically in general practice should be available so that counselling skills learned can be adapted for the setting. For example, much of the work will be short term. The development of training practices for counsellors to allow them practical experience specifically within these settings is a possibility with contracts made between the training institution, the FHSA and the practice. Thus FHSAs need to make links with training bodies to coordinate placement experience in general practice. However, training institutions also need to be encouraged to develop links with potential employers and provide careers advice to potential counsellors and those in training.

## EVALUATION

In setting up and developing the service, ongoing evaluation is essential. This evaluation needs to occur in order to ensure that the service achieves its aims, primarily from the point of quality. All counsellors working in general practice should consider that evaluation and audit form an essential part of their work and their own professional development. They should be constantly questioning their methods of work so that the time they spend in general practice is used as effectively as possible. For example, is time best spent in one-to-one counselling, in group work, in developing the skills of or supporting other practice members, or in some combination?

Alternatively, different methods of working need to be evaluated and studies of clients' views can be invaluable when examining these methods.

There is also a need for FHSAs to be involved in an evaluation of the service as they have a duty to ensure that the services available are at a certain and consistent standard. Determining that standard is relatively arbitrary at present. There is a need for more long-term studies and more detailed studies of outcome including cost-effectiveness. Different methods of working in general practice need to be researched as well as exploring the role of the counsellor as a resource to the primary care team.

This research needs to be coordinated so that different studies use similar measures of outcome to ensure that inappropriate duplication is minimised. Research in this area is extremely difficult to undertake and researchers need to help one another. Now is the time to fund an academic research centre for counselling in general practice.

## WORKING AS A MEMBER OF THE PRIMARY CARE TEAM

A successful placement of a counsellor in general practice should not only benefit the individual patients seen by the counsellor but also give some benefit to practice members. Other members of the primary health care team (PHCT) will vary in their counselling skills and whether they regard this as a major part of their role. Time needs to be invested by the counsellor in supporting and developing the skills of practice members who are interested in taking on a role in this area. Although other PHCT members may not wish to become more involved, it is still important to develop their skills of identification so that they know when to make referral to others when necessary. Very few team members have the luxury of time to reflect on their practice and yet offering such time could enable PHCT members to function more effectively and feel more supported.

One way of developing services is to develop a practice protocol for the psychological care of their population. This may include developing skills of identification as well as support and management. Simple methods of identification of distress within particularly vulnerable groups (e.g. postnatal, carers, etc.) are being developed for use within the PHCT. For example, many health visitors routinely use a postnatal depression scale to screen all mothers.

The development of a protocol or guidelines may also be of value when members of the PHCT have to make decisions regarding when to refer and who to refer. The overlap between team members (particularly between counsellors, psychologists and community psychiatric nurses) may bring about difficulties, and group discussions of the roles and skills of each profession may help to clarify some of the differences and similarities.

The counsellor can have an important role in the development of a protocol and in encouraging effective methods of communication between the PHCT so that a collaborative approach can be adopted. The future will hopefully allow us to develop methods of practice to promote good mental health, both for the practice population and for the PHCT itself.

The future is full of opportunities, building on the foundations which have been laid over the last two decades. It is crucial, however, that guidelines are developed for the employment of counsellors in primary care and moves made towards determining a standard. We must evaluate the skills a counsellor brings to the PHCT and explore different modes of working. But most importantly, we must give more access to a service that, for many people, can enable them to deal with their difficulties and live their lives more resourcefully.

## REFERENCES

Corney, R. and Thomas, R. (1992) 'A survey of GPs' views towards interprofessional collaboration' (in preparation).

Curtis-Jenkins, G. (1991) *So you Want to Start a Counselling Service in your Practice?*, Counselling in Primary Care Trust, Suite 3a, Majestic House, High Street, Staines TW18 4DG.

Jewell, T. (1992) *The Introduction of a Counsellor into Two General Practices*, Unpublished report, Cambridge Health Authority.

# Referral forms and counselling questionnaire

*Roslyn Corney and Annalee Curran*

**Referral form – to be filled in by the referral agent**


**Name of referrer**   ...................................................................................

**Name of the counsellor**   ...........................................................................

**Name of patient**   ..................................................................................

   Address:   ...................................................................................

               ...................................................................................

   Telephone No.   ............................................................................


**Assessment of the problem**




**Reason for referral**




**Expectation of outcome from counselling**




**Patient's motivation to be helped**

| highly motivated | some motivation | mixed feelings | little motivation | probably will refuse help |
|---|---|---|---|---|

**Initial details – to be filled in by the counsellor** (page 1)

**Details of patient/client referred**

**Name of practice** ...........................................................................

**Name of patient** ............................................................................

**Name of counsellor** .......................................................................

**Please underline appropriate category**

| **Sex** | | Male | Female | Couple |
|---|---|---|---|---|

**Age** ................................ (please fill in)

**Marital status**

| Single | Married/ cohabiting | Widowed | Separated | Divorced |
|---|---|---|---|---|

(please indicate current state e.g. if divorced but now cohabiting, underline cohabiting)

| **Age & sex of children living with subject** (only if client is an adult) | None | | | |
|---|---|---|---|---|
| | 1) | M/F | 5) | M/F |
| | 2) | M/F | 6) | M/F |
| | 3) | M/F | | |
| | 4) | M/F | | |

**Work status**

| Full time | Part time | Housewife | Unemployed | Retired | Long-term sick/disabled |
|---|---|---|---|---|---|

**Type of work** .................................................................................

**Work status of spouse**

| Full time | Part time | Housewife | Unemployed | Retired | Long-term sick/disabled |
|---|---|---|---|---|---|

**Type of work** .................................................................................

**Initial details – to be filled in by the counsellor** (continued)

**Name of referral agent** ......................................................................

**Doctor (or referral agent) reason for referral** ...............................

................................................................................................................

................................................................................................................

**Your assessment of problems** .........................................................

................................................................................................................

................................................................................................................

**Motivation to be helped**

| highly motivated | some motivation | mixed feelings | little motivation | refused help |

**Contacts between client and counsellor and assessment of outcome (To be filled in by the counsellor)**

**Name of patient** ...............................................................................

**Closure of case**

| | | | | | |
|---|---|---|---|---|---|
| 1. **No of contacts** | None | 1 | 2 | 3–5 | 6–10 | 11+ |

1. **No of contacts**   None   1   2   3–5   6–10   11+

2. **Total time spent in contact**   None   1hr or less   2hrs   3–5   6–10   11+

3. **Contacts with health care team**

| | | | | | |
|---|---|---|---|---|---|
| No. of contacts with Dr | None | 1 | 2 | 3–5 | 6+ |
| No. of contacts with HV | None | 1 | 2 | 3–5 | 6+ |

No. of contacts with other member
(please specify)   1) ......   None   1   2   3–5   6+
                   2) ......   None   1   2   3–5   6+

4. **Any other agencies contacted or referred to**
(please specify)   ...................................................................
..........................................................................................

5. **No. of sessions client has missed**
(only count those where *no* notice was given)
                   None   1   2   3–5   6+

6. **Reason case closed**
(please tick)      1)   client's request
                   2)   end of specified time
                   3)   pt failed to turn up
                   4)   agreement between client and you
                   5)   referred to (please specify)   ..........
                   6)   your decision
                   7)   other (please specify)   ..................

7. **Changes achieved generally** (including all influences)

Deterioration   No change   Some improvement   Major improvement

8. **Changes achieved mainly through counselling**

Deterioration   No change   Some improvement   Major improvement

9. **Specific areas where you think you have helped**
..........................................................................................
..........................................................................................
..........................................................................................

**To be filled in by the client**

**Counselling questionnaire**

Please tick the appropriate box or answer in your own words as required. There are no right or wrong answers to these questions. Your replies are *confidential* and *will not be relayed* back to the counsellor.

1a. **Who referred you to see the counsellor?**
(Tick appropriate box)

Doctor
Health Visitor
Practice Nurse
Receptionist
Yourself

b. **If you referred yourself, how did you hear about counselling?**

from the practice leaflet
from the doctor
from someone else

(please specify ) .................................................................

c. **How did you feel about being referred to the counsellor?**
(tick one or more appropriate boxes)

would have preferred to carry on seeing doctor
was anxious/nervous about seeing someone else
felt hopeful that counselling would help
wanted to talk to a 'new' person
doubtful about usefulness of counselling

2. **What did you think your problems were at that time?**
(tick one or more boxes)

| Housing | | Depression | |
| Financial | | Relationship problems | |
| Physical illness | | Family problems | |
| Employment | | Confusion about life and the future | |
| Anxiety | | Thought you were going mad | |

Others (please specify) ...........................................

**What did you think your main problem was?**

.................................................................................
.................................................................................

**3a. Did you find your visit/s to the counsellor useful?**

(please tick most appropriate box)

| YES | UNSURE | NO |
|-----|--------|-----|
| ☐ | ☐ | ☐ |

**b. Did you find it easy to talk to the counsellor?**

| YES | UNSURE | NO |
|-----|--------|-----|
| ☐ | ☐ | ☐ |

**c. Did you think you had enough time to explain your problems to the counsellor?**

| YES | UNSURE | NO |
|-----|--------|-----|
| ☐ | ☐ | ☐ |

**d. Do you think the counsellor understood your problems and feelings?**

| YES | UNSURE | NO |
|-----|--------|-----|
| ☐ | ☐ | ☐ |

**4. Did counselling help you in any of the following ways:**

a) getting you to work out how to solve your problems

| YES | UNSURE | NO |
|-----|--------|-----|
| ☐ | ☐ | ☐ |

b) giving you relief by being able to talk about your problem/s

| YES | UNSURE | NO |
|-----|--------|-----|
| ☐ | ☐ | ☐ |

c) helping you cope with your feelings

| YES | UNSURE | NO |
|-----|--------|-----|
| ☐ | ☐ | ☐ |

d) helping you to change within yourself

| YES | UNSURE | NO |
|-----|--------|-----|
| ☐ | ☐ | ☐ |

e) helping you to understand yourself better

| YES | UNSURE | NO |
|-----|--------|-----|
| ☐ | ☐ | ☐ |

f) aiding change with your partner or other family members

| YES | UNSURE | NO |
|-----|--------|-----|
| ☐ | ☐ | ☐ |

g) improving communication between yourself and your partner or other

| YES | UNSURE | NO |
|-----|--------|-----|
| ☐ | ☐ | ☐ |

h) helping you sort out any sexual difficulties

| YES | UNSURE | NO |
|-----|--------|-----|
| ☐ | ☐ | ☐ |

i) giving you a clearer picture of who you are

| YES | UNSURE | NO |
|-----|--------|-----|
| ☐ | ☐ | ☐ |

j) giving you a clearer picture of the future

| YES | UNSURE | NO |
|-----|--------|-----|
| ☐ | ☐ | ☐ |

**5. Did counselling help you in any other way?**
Please write here any other ways in which you were helped

..................................................................................................
..................................................................................................
..................................................................................................

**6a. Would you have liked a different sort of help?**

| | YES | UNSURE | NO |
|---|-----|--------|-----|
| Tablets from the doctor | ☐ | ☐ | ☐ |
| More practical help | | | |
| More advice on what to do | | | |
| Being referred to another agency or hospital | ☐ | ☐ | ☐ |

**b. Would you have liked to change the counselling sessions in any way?**
(please tick appropriate box/boxes)

| | YES | UNSURE | NO |
|---|-----|--------|-----|
| More sessions | ☐ | ☐ | ☐ |
| Longer sessions | | | |
| Shorter sessions | | | |
| Less sessions | ☐ | ☐ | ☐ |

**c. Do you have any suggestions on how it could have been more helpful?**
Please write here

..................................................................................................
..................................................................................................
..................................................................................................

7a. **How much do you think you have changed as a result of counselling?**

(Tick appropriate box)

| A great deal of change for the better | Change for the better | No change | Change for the worse | A great deal of change for the worse |
|:---:|:---:|:---:|:---:|:---:|
| ☐ | ☐ | ☐ | ☐ | ☐ |

b. **How did your problems change as a result of counselling?**

|  | Better | Same | Worse |
|---|:---:|:---:|:---:|
| Housing | ☐ | ☐ | ☐ |
| Financial | ☐ | ☐ | ☐ |
| Physical illness | ☐ | ☐ | ☐ |
| Employment | ☐ | ☐ | ☐ |
| Anxiety | ☐ | ☐ | ☐ |
| Depression | ☐ | ☐ | ☐ |
| Relationship problems | ☐ | ☐ | ☐ |
| Family problems | ☐ | ☐ | ☐ |
| Confusion about life and the future | ☐ | ☐ | ☐ |
| Thought you were going mad | ☐ | ☐ | ☐ |

Others (please specify)

......................................................

......................................................

......................................................

| | Better | Same | Worse |
|---|:---:|:---:|:---:|
| | ☐ | ☐ | ☐ |

8a. **Were you happy about the way the counselling ended?**

|  | YES | UNSURE | NO |
|---|:---:|:---:|:---:|
| Did you feel ready to stop seeing the counsellor? | ☐ | ☐ | ☐ |
| Would you have liked to go on seeing the counsellor? | ☐ | ☐ | ☐ |
| Were you relieved to stop seeing the counsellor? | ☐ | ☐ | ☐ |
| Did you feel the ends had been tied up? | ☐ | ☐ | ☐ |
| Did you feel you could come back to the counsellor if you needed to? | ☐ | ☐ | ☐ |

b. **Why did you stop seeing the counsellor?**
   (Tick appropriate box)
   We agreed to end the counselling
   I decided to end the counselling
   The counsellor decided to end the counselling
   I stopped going
   I went to see someone else

9. **What are/were your overall feelings about counselling?**
   Please write here
   .............................................................................................
   .............................................................................................
   .............................................................................................

# Name index

Anderson, S.A. 25, 27, 32
Ashurst, P.M. 35, 41

Balestrieri, M. 41
Balint, M. 3
Ball, V. 97–102
Barr, J. 26
Beauchamp, T.H. 46
Blacker, C.V.R. 9
British Association for
  Counselling (BAC) 2, 18, 22, 58
British Psychological Society 99
Brown, G.W. 9, 13

Catalan, J. 40
Chester, R. 67
Childress, J.F. 46
Clare, A.W. 9
Cooper, B. 13
Corney, R. 1–6, 31–44, 36, 89–96,
  97–102, 103–14
*Counselling in General Practice* 60
Counselling in Primary Care
  Trust 98
Counselling and Psychotherapy
  Resources Directory 59
Croft-Jeffreys, C. 10
Curran, A. 75–88, 103–14

Department of Health 1
District Health Authority 2

Earll, L. 39
Eastwood, M.R. 13

Egan, A.S. 20, 21

Family Health Service
  Authorities (FHSAs) 3, 64, 68,
  97–8
Family Practitioner Committees
  (FPCs) 2, 3

General Practice Research Unit 7
Gillon, R. 45–55
Goldberg, D.P. 11

Harris, T.O. 13, 17, 22
Hasler, J.C. 25, 27, 32
Heath, V. 25
Henderson, S. 13
Higgs, R. 75–88
Huxley, P. 11

Institute of Psychiatry 7
Irving, J. 25, 56–66

Jenkins, R. 1–6, 45–55

Kant, I. 48
Kincey, J. 39
Knight, L. 18

McLeod, J. 3, 24
Mann, A. 7–16, 13
Marsh, G.N. 2, 26, 67–74
Martin, E. 28, 33
Martin, P.M.L. 33
Mill, J.S. 48

# Subject index